An H in the Heart

An H in the Heart

bpNichol

A Reader

selected by

George Bowering

and

Michael Ondaatje

M&S

THE MODERN CANADIAN POETS SERIES

Canadian Cataloguing in Publication Data

Nichol, B. P., 1944-1988
An H in the heart: a reader

(The Modern Canadian Poets)
Poems.
ISBN 0-7710-6814-X

I. Bowering, George, 1935-   . II. Ondaatje, Michael,
1943-   . III. Title. IV. Series.

PS8527.I32H16 1994 C811'.54 C94-931931-7
PR9199.3.N53I16 1994

Typesetting by M&S, Toronto

The publishers acknowledge the support of the Canada Council
and the Ontario Arts Council for their publishing program.

The support of the Government of Ontario through the
Ministry of Culture and Communications is acknowledged.

Printed and bound in Canada. The paper used in this book
is acid-free.

Author photo: Michael Ondaatje

McClelland & Stewart Inc.
The Canadian Publishers
481 University Avenue
Toronto, Ontario
M5G 2E9

1 2 3 4 5   98 97 96 95 94

A

LAKE

A

LANE

A

LINE

A

LONE

To mark the occasion of the April 30, 1994, dedication of bpNichol Lane behind Coach House Press (Barrie Nichol was part of Coach House for over twenty years), Stan Bevington and David Smith collaborated on setting the concrete poem above into the concrete pavement outside Coach House. Stan did a preview on the Macintosh screen and ran phototypsetting letters at final size – about eight feet of poem. David cut out the letters to make a stencil, sprayed the poem onto the concrete, and chiselled the words out with a diamond-bit router and a diamond-blade saw. Stan Bevington is the founder and continuing genius of Coach House Press, still located on bpNichol Lane, though Coach House Publishing has moved. Every day he goes out and fills the LAKE with water.

Contents

Introduction

by George Bowering

When bpNichol worked for his keep in the basement of the library at the University of Toronto, he would feel the weight of all those floors full of books above him. What would be the use of adding another book or two to those millions of heavy volumes, he would think. So he decided to do something different. He did something different for a scant quarter of a century. While he lived, he was the prince of difference. When he was taken from us so early, everyone said things will never be the same.

That is to say, bpNichol was always trying to escape the book. He got out of the basement and out of the university and became the syllabus. He became, as everyone points out, our main polymath. When he made books, he made books that tried to get out of books. He made songs and cartoons and TV shows. He made operas and computer disks and a bloody fool of himself. For love. For art. For us.

It is really hard, when you are writing about bpNichol, to stay away from hagiography. It is tempting to essay word play and uncommendable puns. He was a wonderful teacher and a terrible influence. You will find a lot of writers who will admit that bp saved them from despair and stupidity. In my own case, it was too late. He delighted in reciting a dreadful line in a poem I have been trying to forget for decades. To get even, I often recite one of his early poems in my university classes. But it doesn't work; the poem is too damned good.

So what do we do? We try to edit a selected Nichol. Worse than that, we try to do it in a book. Worse even than that, we try to do it in a book that is not two thousand pages long. So in compiling such a text, we make the inevitable apologies and excuses: in this volume there are no tipped-in computer disks; there are no LP records; there are no children's books, no TV puppets, no song-and-dance numbers, no concrete poems made of real concrete, no body painting, no multilingual mime. Most of bp's modes and genres are not here in this book we have tried to make.

"You Too, Nicky" was printed as a "card" for Christmas 1989, the year after Barrie's death, and is much asked after. Except for that, no selections from *The Martyrology* are here. Thanks to the brave Coach House Press, that enormous ten-book poem is in print again. The decision to restrict a bp sampler almost entirely to non-*Martyrology* material was perhaps the easiest decision for the editors to make. Another was to include the entirety of *Organ Music,* the last bpNichol book to come out before his death.

There were, of course, many hard decisions generally when it came to exclusions. When it came to inclusions, we took into consideration the dimensions of bp's garden of voices, and contacted various writers in his life, asking for suggestions. They gave us the titles of their favourite works. You couldn't make a book like this any other way. This method resulted in a manuscript that became heavy enough to cause anxiety in any basement librarian.

But somewhere in *The Martyrology* the voice says "everything is part of something else." That can mean that once you have begun, you have to read everything. Or it can mean that once you have read something, you have read part of everything. The good thing about being in a labyrinth is that you get to make the choice of direction. You have to make a lot of turns, but that is what verse means. That is what history teaches. As Nichol put it in his note to the fifth book of his deconstructive epic: "As a reader you can continue thru the chain of ideas you're already following, or you can choose, at different points, to diverge." bp was always trying to keep the reader active, awake in the language.

It's not easy being a reader, unless you are reading the same thing over and over. This is impossible to do with a bpNichol text. This is so partly because he loved **h** in itself, not just as the thing between **t** and **e**, and it is so because Nichol is a highly moral writer, perhaps more so than any of his contemporaries. His writing about saints was not just a clever trope; he was interested in the good of the intellect. His song, even if sung on a Saturday morning TV show, was a hymn. A hymn to be heard.

Perhaps what I have been trying to say is that bpNichol was a preternaturally generous human being, giving of himself and his talent to a whole world of writers and other people. Commentators often bring up Lewis Hyde's idea of the gift economy when they are discussing Nichol's writing and teaching and editing. He gave his time and he (gave his) art to a thousand younger and older poets, and he gave his writing to a network of little magazines and small literary presses in the poetry diaspora. In a sense it is an un-Nicholesque thing to do, this making of a book of Barrie's writing to be published by a major publisher, even though the publisher is based in Barrie's Toronto and Canada.

So we had a meeting and talked it out, a small group of us Nichol miners and the heroine of his poems, his wife, Ellie. The questions were all put and the arguments were all gently made. Would bp have approved? Isn't it about time that a wide distribution was made aboveground? Can this bpNichol reader coexist with the books produced with such nice attention by the non-profit small presses? We decided that we wanted for Barrie what he never asked for himself – a hefty collection to be placed in the mainstream. No one will ever read it and consider bpNichol a merchant of sameness. His devoted readers will never turn away. Poetry readers and teachers who have somehow missed his quarter-century of invention will find something that might lead them into the labyrinth. Okay, said Ellie.

It has been a lot of effort, this gathering of sometimes

fugitive texts, this choosing to chop out beautiful and successful experiments. I urge readers to put on their work clothes and negotiate the mazes they will find in heroic first-edition bookstores. Probably, when they locate a copy of *Six Fillious* (1978), they will ask why it wasn't included in the reader. Welcome to the club. Keep reading.

So the editors would like to thank all the publishers and typesetters of all the magazines and presses that have given us back bpNichol's work and voice. Thank you to everyone from the other arts who gave us Nichol in music halls, TV studios, dance palaces, and art galleries. A blank cheque of gratitude to Stan Dragland, who worked on this book with more than editorial eyes. We would also like to thank everyone who talked to us about this new book, especially Ellie Nichol, and including Irene Niechoda, Steve McCaffery, Lola Lemire Tostevin, Frank Davey, Paul Dutton, Roy Miki, Doug Barbour, Charlene Diehl-Jones, Diane Martin, Victor Coleman, nicky drumbolis, jwcurry. If we have somehow forgotten to mention you, write your name here:

An H in the Heart

YOU TOO, NICKY

I

All of us are born out of someone. Too many of us spend a lifetime tied to that moment or trying to live it down. But family, what you came from, what came before you, lives in the body like an organ you only know the shape of thru x-rays or textbooks. Who were they, really, those early ones who suffer from the diffusion of histories lived with no importance given to writing them down? We, all of us, move forward thru time at the tip of a family, a genealogy, whose history & description disappears behind us.

'You too, Nicky,' a friend said to me, 'none of us ever escapes our families.' And restless, as i have been, tired, as i am now, feeling some sort of longing which can only be satisfied by moving & is never satisfied by standing still, i took off with Ellie in the autumn of 1979 to visit, revisit, both our families. Among the luggage we carried was a notebook i had kept in 1969 when i had last driven west. In its opening pages i found this poem:

the dead
porcupine
                    decapitated by
the speeding cars
                         & the bleak stone
landscapes
            going home(?)
thru the Sault

                    it is
a country as wide as dreams are
full of the half-formed
unsuspected
                    ruthlessness
around the corner of things
the smooth hum of the car
carrying the far strangers ahead of us

nothing is as it seems

the partly known truth entices

we are forbidden to pass till the future is seen

it is as if
            hands
                        reached out & touched us
as they were meant to do

the grey clouds turned over &
their backs were blue

II

You have plans but so many of them don't work out. You
have dreams, tho you do not mean the dreams you wake
from, troubled or happy, but visions rather, glimpses of
some future possibility everything in you wishes to make
real. We drove west but the poems I'd planned to write
barely occurred. A few fragments here & there – Edmon-
ton, Blue River, Vancouver – cities & places I had visited &
written from before. By the time we got back Ellie was

pregnant and much of the shape of our lives together changed. Even tho our son died stillborn, or because of it perhaps, our lives changed absolutely. It is the kind of moment of which one tends to say 'something deepened between us' and yet that notion of depth seems in itself shallow, lacking as it does an attention to the details of the dailiness between you, the actual exchanges that comprise living. Other poems occurred but nothing of what was planned. We came out of families, came together and within two years of that trip had begun a family of our own. Except the family was there before we began. We were part of it. Became part of it again. Despite what I had once intended. Unplotted, unplanned, undreamt of. It continued. It began.

III

There is some larger meditation that seems obvious. An inference or moral perhaps. I only know the poem unfolds in front of me, in spite of me, more in control than me. Its not that the poem has a mind of its own but that poetry is its own mind, a particular state you come to, achieve.

Sometimes i talk too much of it, like a magician explaining his best trick and you see after all he is only human. Which is what I wish to be, am, only human.

Certain phrases like that, that hover on the edge of cliché, seem like charms to me & i clutch them to my chest. And the real magic, which is what the language can achieve, remains a mystery the charm connects you to.

> it is not so much that
> images recur

but that life
repeats itself
& the lights of
Vancouver say
shine
even when lines aren't there to be written

Only human, only a skill you've managed to achieve. And if
the writing is evocative it is only so thru evocation. Which is
partly syntax, partly mystery.

IV

what is smaller than us?

what is more futile than
our wars and treacheries

we are all dying
every day walking closer to the grave
the sword and the bomb and age accompany us

what are the great themes but those we cannot name
properly

what are the minor notes but
our lives

here amidst the flickering oil wells
among the fields now emptied from harvest

our lives

all that really is ours

V

Of course I repeat myself, phrases, insist certain contents
over & over.

> driving thru the smoke of the forest fires
> Blue River to Kamloops
> sun not yet visible over the mountaintops

Of course I had driven that road before. Others. Corre-
spondences. You build up a vocabulary of shared experi-
ences, constants you draw on tho you cannot depend on
them.

> between the still standing trees
> the smoke   the mist
> down into the valleys

Of course I am *aware* of what I am doing, not aware. Of
course there are such contradictions in living.

VI

We have our infatuations, our cloudings of the mind.
People, ideas, things. We have our fevers that drive others
from us, afraid of the shrill quality in our voice.

> we are pushed here   there
> 'driven' is what we say
> and the i is lost

And if i tries to retain a kind of loyalty to ideas, not blindly,
but allowing them, always, to evolve under the scrutiny that
time permits, it is simply that struggle with constancy, to
stick with what makes sense until it no longer makes sense,
to not be swayed by infatuation's blind calling. It is what

binds books together, these motifs and concerns, the trace
of a life lived, a mind.

> in the rooms you live in
> other people's books line your shelves
>
> the traces of their lives
> their minds
>
> too

VII

something of that is what family is. other minds enter, other
lives you pledge a constancy to.

there are other journeys, other poems, other plans that do
not realize themselves.

living among family you are changed. it is the way your
vocabulary increases. you occupy certain nouns, are caught
up in the activity of certain verbs, adverbs, adjectives. syntax
too. tone.

the language comes alive as you come alive and the real mys-
teries remain.

> outside the window
> the rumble of other journeys
> planes, trains, cars passing
> the feet of friends or strangers echo the unseen concrete
>
> the blind is white under its horizontal ribbing
>
> the world enters
>
> your ear

```
±  @  #  $  %  ¢  &  *  (  )     +
1  2  3  4  5  6  7  8  9  0  ‾-  =

Q  W  E  R  T  Y  U  I  O  P  ¼
q  w  e  r  t  y  u  i  o  p  ½

A  S  D  F  G  H  J  K  L  :  "
a  s  d  f  g  h  j  k  l  ;  '

Z  X  C  V  B  N  M  ,  .  ?
z  x  c  v  b  n  m  ,  .  /
```

_____

*any possible permutation
of all listed elements

4 MOODS

1) The Friendliness of the Alphabet
abcdefgHIjklmnopqrstuvwxyz

2) The Denial of the Alphabet
abcdefghijklmNOpqrstuvwxyz

3) The Sanctimoniousness of the Alphabet
abcdefghijklmnopqrSTuvwxyz

4) The Self-Centredness of the Alphabet
abcdefghIjklmnopqrstuvwxyz

SANS SERIF—NOVELTY

Radiant Medium ABCDEF
Radiant Medium: 12 14 18 24 30 36 42 48 60 72

Radiant Bold Extra Condensed ABCDEF
Radiant Bold Extra Condensed: 14 18 24 30 36 42 48

Radiant Bold Condensed ABCDE
Radiant Bold Condensed: 12 14 18 24 30 36 42 48 60 7

Radiant Bold ABCDEFGI
Radiant Bold: 12 14 18 24 30 36 42 48 60 72

Radiant Heavy ABCDEF
Radiant Heavy: 12 14 18 24 30 36 42 48 60 72

FAMILIAR

drove into the country for hours
roads we'd never been before

shelburne

grand valley

ellie & me
driving down till we came to
nichol township
wellington county

& i thot
"i am home"

not knowing where i was
or where home might be

as cabot
in   1497
discovered the west was
good for fishing
                    lief the lucky had
500 years earlier
found such grapes he
thot it was the gods' home

                              as hunters had
before him
                found the hunting good &

come thru alaska

          into america

& the mass of land
which was said to lie
between africa &
some western shore
promoted the spread of culture from
egypt to the olmecs

the lack of substantial fact
makes history the memory of
an amnesiac

makes anything his
who works it with his hands

& such lies as are made myths

                  accepted
as planned

"this was in south dakota"
near iroquois

          my great grandpa &
grandma leigh

          broke 40 acres
1885

     near ed fry
& old jimmy davis who lived in a cave in the hill
(the only shelter he could build)

gave birth to
their first child (a girl)

florence leigh
stayed on a pillow till she died
3 months later

"what god gives
god takes away"

& great grandpa caspar
with his one arm
broke the ground for her grave

"o lord please save this child from harm"

my great aunt maggie
married four times

the first was a man died of tb
his name was max tease

the second (a butcher) shot himself
accidentally

& when she met Merry   hell well
he was number three
                    & swept her off her feet

it was almost a year before he ran away
took all the money she'd managed to save
& left her

at least he didn't die

i can almost hear maggie heaving a sigh of relief

then stepping out the door
into the arms of number four

june 12 1911

walter workman
wife & two children

1911 broke 3 acres cropped none
1912 broke 9 acres cropped 3
1913 broke 11 acres cropped 12
1914 broke 17 acres cropped 23

worked on a farm south of viscount to support himself

under livestock listed
1 cow

my father was raised in goodwater
faded photo of him standing by a car
an old fur coat
he looks 15
his sister marie is at the wheel
his father beside her

the street is dusty

the land is flat

somewhere below his feet
two oceans meet

one of salt water
one of sweet

we know there are wells

in ten more years it will be 1929
shortly after that the drought
the good water dries up
noone eats well

he & my mother are married
their first child dies
they never manage to get her picture taken

none of this is there in the photo

it is so obvious his smiling face is unaware of history
the future force it was/is/will be

all my life having searched in the west
to discover the name in a book
                              robert nichol
1806
       how he had owned two lots 6 & 7
6 concessions over from
                              yonge street
in the township of east gwillimbury
york county
& to know nothing more
is (as they say)
to find new mysteries in the east

(these lines stretch back   farther than i remember
farther than i've been able to go

break awkwardly   in the middle
like a poem

                    or a son
born at the wrong time

the workman & the nichol line
passing thru ontario
a half a century
before they finally met

in a hotel
on a corner
in plunkett)

robert nichol
came to america   1860
with his brothers   john & hugh

started a flax mill
near the city of salem

& then
                    when the civil war was thru
went north
                    into ontario

did he know that a robert nichol had been thru there before

that in any history
there is nothing new

only a few things
rearranged

paths which cross

worlds (which grow smaller)

different points of view

like every other crazy robert nichol
going into something over his head

named a township after him
just because he'd been brock's friend

commissary in the war of blunders
one of the natives brock never trusted

driving his horse & carriage
thru the dark to lundy's lane

plunged over the bluffs at queenston
pulling everything down behind him

backing those idiots dickson and clarke
used him to rob the government blind

trying to be a man who spoke for
his people and his time

raised the question of immigration of
the government land preserve

fought the clergy reserves
sucked in again by speculators

sailed over the cliff walls
screaming lost in the falls' thunder

never stopped to wonder who his friends really were

picked him up off the shore &
laid him to earth

for what it's worth

did i tell you bout my uncle fred
                                        fell
head over dead
into the paddle wheel of a mississippi steamer

or so it's said

never found a trace of his body

nobody knows for sure to this day
except to say he died

on that ship

on that night

who cares for history?

it is his story
or her story or
the story of someone
noone knows

                              & now that you know
what do you know?

                            questions

always it seems there are questions

once there was a man emigrated from england   passed thru
ontario into minnesota   married and raised some
    children
then was gored by a bull

that is history

that's how his story goes

name names
place places

put your history
in your head

bury the dead
with honour

honour the living
with love

& when your time comes
it comes

when you are gone you are gone
& leave behind
a son or
a daughter or
noone

LOVE SONG 6
For Ellie on her birthday (November 19/73, 12:02 a.m.)

all the ways that i had thot of loving
filled as i can be with such conceits
disappear in the face of you
the place you do take in my heart

all the awkwardness that i feel in phrasing
poems that speak of my loving for you
caught as they do catch in a moment's saying
so that i feel embarrassed or arrogant
hesitating where i should be sure
are nothing when i hold you
unable to speak
   reach over the years of our separate growing
older together
     measured in time
we note startled
no closer to knowing "what love is"
except that respect
     that continual wonder
i still dissemble before
more in love with you than ever

CATCHING FROGS
for LeRoy Gorman

jar din

SKETCH FOR A BOTANICAL DRAWING
FOR THOMAS A. CLARK

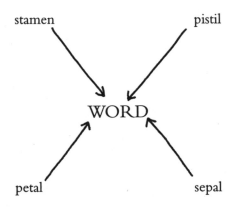

CONTENT (WITH SMALL PRESS RUNS)

1

ink

(in like a lake)

fin flynn

        small connections

snail like
a lack of
S

     cargo nailed down

town

2

reader ship

& the wavering
up & down
200 to 500 to seven hundred

fifty and one
thou

sand and
sea

sail or
steam

sea/m

3

many or one 'r

any on board at all
points

forwards & backwards

type cast or
photographed

paging

4

hello

out there

reading me

listening with the third eye

hi

dream & commentaries as a probable source
(with additional research including PROBABLE
SYSTEMS 30)

Friday August 17th, 1973

    dreamt i'd returned to wildwood park in winnipeg.
they'd torn down all the houses and trees in the centre of the
u-shaped section we used to live in, including our old
house, and covered the whole thing with gravel. at the bot-
tom of the u an apartment building was going up. i started
crying & screaming because they were going to destroy the
trees and the parkland between the u-sections.

commentary 1: poem (august 17th, 1973)

drove east thru the kawarthas toward verona
burleigh falls behind us
where i thot i saw the drowned child
feet & arms wedged beneath the rocks

awaking that morning
dreams of the red river flood
where we'd lived   H-section   wildwood park
lifetime pursuits explained
                      mysterious other train of thot
drawing me east out of the dreamed landscape
"was" is all i "saw"

H circa 1950
i can never go back again
before H

A to G
winnipeg manitoba
w in m
      i in H
its section?

"look" for the big H   Harvey comics
didackdick tracing   passages of a thot
the facts stack backwards
                      the connections
origins of a quest
was that how it was when they wandered east
shields emblazoned with the family crest
under the grail's holy influence?
the children who had gone before them
                    to be sold into slavery or
dead beside the highway
where the next crusade would find them

child of H
children of Holy Matrimony
M into 3
Holy Trinity of suffering
host out of Ghost
fed nothing for their vision but lies
God's host betrayed
it was lost love they thot to find

despair thru the laurentians
north towards noranda
the chaos is man's
the perfect plan is not planned
that space that line run parallel yet meet

H
   crude symbol of the bridging
a re-perception of what was once unitas

I

   H

     S

commentary 2: autobiographical note

in 1950 i was living with my mother, father, sister and two brothers in H-section, one of a number of u-shaped sections in an area of Winnipeg called Wildwood Park. in the spring of that year, the Red River flooded its banks, creating in the process a major disaster, and we, and thousands of others like us, were forced to move out until the disaster had passed and the clean-up that followed was finished. i have a vague memory of my Mom, my sister and me being carried away in a boat across areas i was used to walking over. we went to live with relatives, first in Saskatoon and then in Calgary.

H-section was where i first learned my ABC's, and one of the things i learned at the same time was how to find my way home. if i was walking from one direction i knew that right after G-section was H-section and H was where home was. if i was walking from another direction i knew that I came just after H so that H-section had to be the next one i'd come to. and of course i could always cut thru the middle of the Park and jump from one letter to another in all kinds of patterns, just as a way of getting home.

i hated the period when we were up-rooted, sleeping in borrowed beds under cramped conditions. it was, as they say, traumatic. and i was over-joyed when we finally moved back, six months later. we got our dad to show us how high the flood water had risen (to just below the window of my sister's and mine's second floor bedroom) and then had him nail a little wooden donkey to the spot to mark what had happened. sometimes my sister and i would try to imagine the house under all that water, as tho we had lived there, in it (under it), thru the whole flood.

but something happened to me after that flood. when the water receded i had changed. i had become H obsessed. i collected the Hardy Boys and Harvey Comics (whose slogan was "look for the Big H!" & who published, among other titles, *Dick Tracy Comics*). i loved Baby Huey and the comic my brother drew "SUPERHOG" (which circulated widely for a number of years in its single hand-drawn version and then disappeared). H. i couldn't get enough of it. and of course it was still H-section and, for a time, Home. all of which i forgot or, at least, never connected with my adult interest, until August 17th, 1973, when i had the above dream, me with my (part) German roots, discovering the origin in my Hunconscious of one of the I's obsessions.

bill bissett is lone attendee at the Hundred Mile House's Syntactic Drift and Other Mush Colloquium, February 1988. #8 in the collectible series on our Lively Literary Legacy.

DADA LAMA

to the memory of Hugo Ball

I

hweeeee
hweeeee
hyonnnn
hyonnnn

hweeeee
hweeeee
hyonnnn
hyonnnn

tubadididdo
tubadididdo
hyon
hyon

tubadididdo
tubadididdo
hyon
hyon

ffffffffffffffffffffffffftsssssssss
ffffffffffffffffffffffffitsssssssss
ffffffffffffffffffffffflitsssssssss

hyonnnnnn
         unh
hyonnnnnn
         unh

2

eeeeeeeeeeeeeeeeeeeeeeeeeee
EEEEEEEEEEEEEEEEEEE
eeeeeeeeeeeeeeeeeeeeeeeeeee

EEEEEEEEEEEEEEEEEEE
eeeeeeeeeeeeeeeeeeeeeeeeeeee
EEEEEEEEEEEEEEEEEEEE

eeeeeeeeeeeeeeeeeeeeeeeeeeee
EEEEEEEEEEEEEEEEEEEE
eeeeeeeeeeeeeeeeeeeeeeeeeeee

3

oudoo doan doanna
tinna limn limn
la leen
untloo lima
limna doo doo

dee du deena
deena dee du
deena deena
dee du deena

ah-ooo runtroo
lintle leave lipf
lat lina tanta
tlalum cheena
ran tron tra troo

deena dee du
deena deena
dee du deena
deena dee du

da dee di do du
deena
     deena

4

AAAAAAAAAAAAAAAAAAA
aaaaaaaaaaaaaaaaaaaaaaaaaaaaaaaa
AAAAAAAAAAAAAAAAAAAA

aaaaaaaaaaaaaaaaaaaaaaaaaaaaaaaa
AAAAAAAAAAAAAAAAAAAA
aaaaaaaaaaaaaaaaaaaaaaaaaaaaaaaa

AAAAAAAAAAAAAAAAAAAA
aaaaaaaaaaaaaaaaaaaaaaaaaaaaaaaa
AAAAAAAAAAAAAAAAAAAA

5

tlic
tloc

tlic tloc
tlic tloc

tlic tloc tlic
tloc tlic tloc

tlic tloc tlic tloc
tlic tloc tlic tloc

tlic tloc tlic tloc tlic
tloc tlic tloc tlic tloc

tlic tloc tlic tloc tlic tloc
tlic tloc tlic tloc tlic tloc

tlic tloc tlic tloc tlic
tloc tlic tloc tlic tloc

tlic tloc tlic tloc
tlic tloc tlic tloc

tlic tloc tlic
tloc tlic tloc

tlic tloc
tlic tloc

tlic
tloc

6

wwwwwwwwwwwwwwwwwwwwwwwwwww
mmmmmmmmmmmmmmmmmmmmmmmmmmm
wwwwwwwwwwwwwwwwwwwwwwwwwww
mmmmmmmmmmmmmmmmmmmmmmmmmmm

Wwwwwwwwwwwwwwwwwwwwwwwwww
Mmmmmmmmmmmmmmmmmmmmmmmmmm
Wwwwwwwwwwwwwwwwwwwwwwwwww
Mmmmmmmmmmmmmmmmmmmmmmmmmm

WWWWWWWWWWWWWWWWWWWWWWWWW
MMMMMMMMMMMMMMMMMMMMMMMMM
WWWWWWWWWWWWWWWWWWWWWWWWW

OUOOOOOOOOOOOOOOOOOOOOOOOOH
MMMMMMMMMMMMMMMMMMMMMMMMMM
OUOOOOOOOOOOOOOOOOOOOOOOOOH
MMMMMMMMMMMMMMMMMMMMMMMMMM

FREEEEEEEEEEEEEEEEEEEEEEEE
EEEAAAAAAAAAAAAAAAAAAAAAAAH
FREEEEEEEEEEEEEEEEEEEEEEEEE
EEEAAAAAAAAAAAAAAAAAAAAAAAH

FREEEEEEEEEEEEEEEEEEEEEEEEE
DUMMMMMMMMMMMMMMMMMMMMMMMM
FREEEEEEEEEEEEEEEEEEEEEEEEE
DUMMMMMMMMMMMMMMMMMMMMMMMM

LAMENT

for d.a. levy who took his life

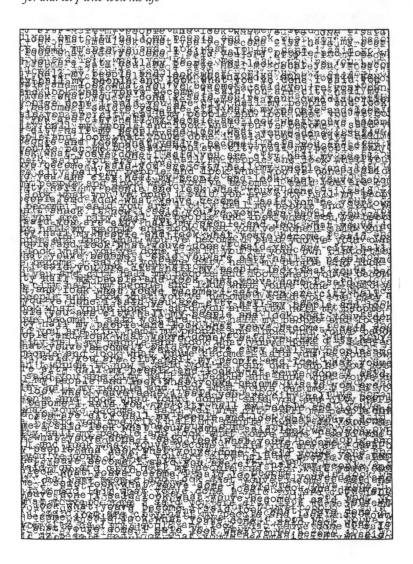

from "**The Plunket Papers**"

we rode the train back west in 54
my dad sister & me
outside of red rock had to stop 12 hours
coz of a slide
                    ran over 2 workers
just after getting under way again

i remember seeing them from the train
the blood & the severed arms
& after we heard the one man died

heading out to plunkett from port arthur
the summer before i turned ten
meeting uncle bill in saskatoon
drove down to my uncle mike's farm
running over this prairie chicken on the way
our faces turned white
thing flopping crazily in the dust

& later
                my sister & me
walked down the road from hun & mike's farm

just the two of us

death all around us

determined to make it
on that last mile to plunkett

st*r

em ty

blob
blob

Bob Cobbing studies Steve Smith's
winning form in the Writer's Forum
Tenth Annual Simultaneous Sound
Sonnet + Suds Sipping Marathon at
the Writer's Forum local in London,
England. #6 in a series of Lively
Literary Lacuna. Why not get them all?

RUTH

Why have I found grace in thine eyes,
that thou shouldest
take knowledge of me,
Seeing I *am* a stranger.

Ruth 2:10

•

tear up our fingers

mend them
with lies

set forth
on real ships
into
an imaginary sea

the shores
vague

      lines

linking my eyes
to my heart's

          patterns

the slanting
shadows
make

44

moving large
above the keys

uncharted, stretching
for miles

into
an imaginary
coast

the waves carry

the torn
& broken body
of the host

•

end
ryme

the final bell
tolled
on a fogbound sea

eternity
a step
to be taken

over

a breath

O breathe!   salt

the lung
stings

fog
clinging
to the rung
note

●

our prayers sealed
in leaky ships

cast off

"will they
return?"

"to me"

          he said

"it is so much
bad
      ryme"

(or rythm)

the pace
always the same

ships sink
or are sent out again

safe in harbor
dreaming
of their faces

fingers entwine
nothingness
takes their names

held   with the same   care

her arms

       her legs

         her hair

Allegory # 6

AN INTERLUDE IN WHICH SAINT RANGLEHOLD ADDRESSES ANYONE WHO'LL LISTEN

I

a light in a tree
a hand in a crowd
memory

whistle

now we will change directions
this time for good

what is the structure of heaven
it is a circle within a circle ad nauseam

if i am to stop & talk to you you must give me reason
i am a busy man

h z y k
l r p t m
u u

2

what is the meaning of meaning

it is whistling when the thunder claps or pissing when it rains

did you get the groceries

i tried but they were closed

when i asked a man to consider theory he said
i will think on it when i have a spare moment

3

despair is an air you sing

sorrow is to row your boat nowhere

h is not t
i is not m

whatever was is & will be again

from "The Other Side of the Room"

this morning the dream will not visit me
awakened to the traffic on cedar avenue
i have driven over the bridges
and am no longer there

the hall is wide
wider than the river that flows &
the sword that is offered
                              i cannot take

                    what holds me now?

it is surely death   head caught in the poem
surely my own life
lost beneath the speeding cars on côte des neiges

remember a time
the lines flowed thru me
simply to be born

                         stare at my watch
losing myself
                 my mind

all that's encompassed ends

all that was song & meaning lost

sound of machinery tossed back from
cold high walls

for dave & denise

SEAQUENCE
for phyllis webb

a new beginning
begging
      for an ending

but nothing

no string
to tie it up
neatly

the fisherman weaves his nets
but cannot spell

the sea
      finds its way thru
into   wells   the farmer digs
praying for rain

major mover is a tide that pulls   steady
till the force is   tidal

and the former casts his runes in despair
fleeing into waves struggle in nets or

carried to well's bottom

to stare up disconsolately
into the face   his seed   begets

●

the sea
a mirror
          the heart skips upon
when thrown carelessly

as words are
                    often
in a poem

          or
as a friend said
" 'love' words are"

cheap
          i said
casting my heart into the sea

all things return to some shore

one searches all one's life
to fill the core's
emptiness

                    waiting

anywhere the tide comes
in

     into

come into me

•

poems

friends give
to friends

      gestures

somehow
to cross
the real world

      of fantasy

into a real world without words

as in the poem
a syllable's discarded
to reveal a real breast

      "the rest
      is
      history"

in a minor key

no music for major mover
that is not his
      hers
eventually

CIRCUS DAYS

gathering
of years

still photos of

        my mother

1930
circus billboard

it was
the greatest show on earth

the greatest show
ever to hit
Plunkett, Saskatchewan

•

remember
as a kid

Casey Brothers
coming to town

hated all that
candy floss

        the rides were
lousy

once around this fucking little track
and that was the roller coaster

we must've spent three dollars there
perverts trying to buy us off with candy floss

i remember
Shaunna Sawin didn't go
coz
     they had such a
lousy show

●

lying on the beach at
Port Dover

         they had
a permanent   arcade

dropped my quarter in
to watch the women
take off
     their clothes &
wrote a poem

        Beach at Port Dover

&
     after that
there was this
sudden storm

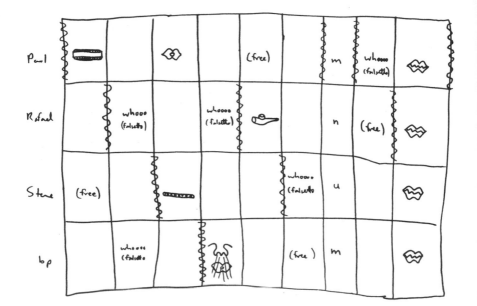

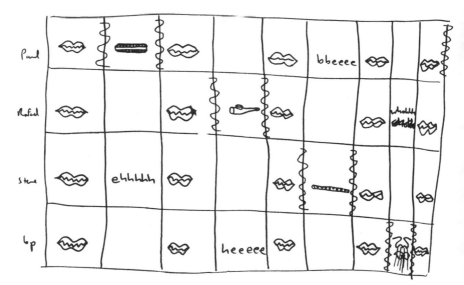

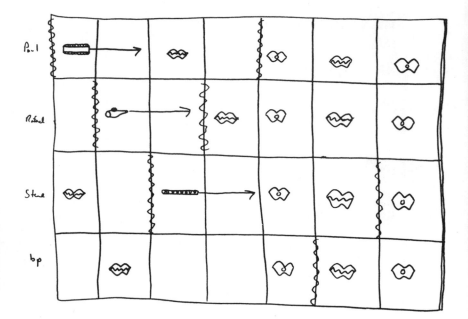

PARTICULAR MUSIC

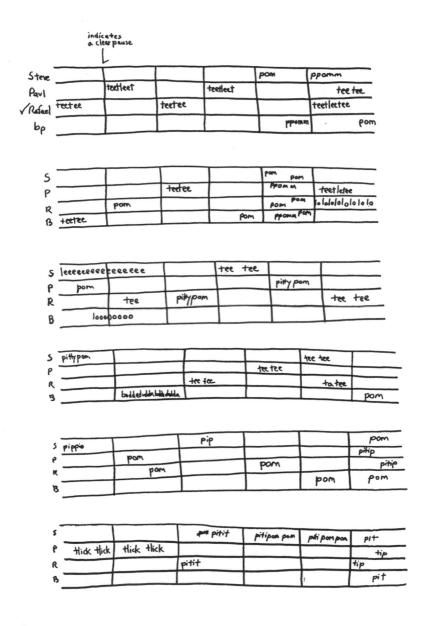

59

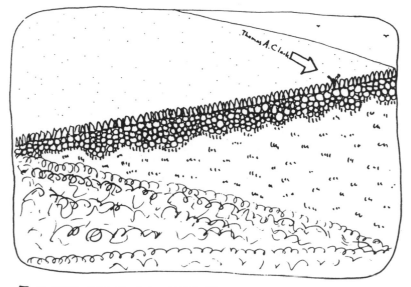

ECSTATIC VICTOR THOMAS A. CLARK IS
SEEN HERE AT VICTORY MOMENT ON ROCKNESS HILL
IN NON-ANNUAL GLOUCESTER FOUND ODE CONTEST.
A LOST BOTTLE OF COLOGNE PROVIDED CLARK WITH
THE CRUCIAL PUN FOR HIS MARCH 31st 1979 TRIUMPH.
OTHER CONTESTANTS INCLUDED LAURIE CLARK, JOHN
FURNIVAL, ASTRID FURNIVAL + FRENCH HOPE HENRI
CHOPIN.
                    #3 in a series of lively literary events

C'MON KIDS! CLIP THEM! SAVE THEM! TRADE THEM!

from "**Catullus poem XXVIII**"

Piss on his committees, cohorts in inanities
apt as sarcasm & as expeditious,
Verani was too optimistic my Fabulle,
who put the geritol in his rum? satisfied? me?! with such
vapid frigid rascals and too listless women?
Damn him as well in tableaus patterned at Lucelli's
expense, dumb monkey, who sucks the mothers'
pretties for refreshment and yells 'Oh –
oh mommy, give me that godly supper –
to taste the trickle in my lips makes you my master'
(said with big eyes, parents being first
cause (such minor nihilistic truths
are farts)). the prick's a noble friend!
the voices of men milking gods with
their teeth are as appropriate as Romulus's remarks.

PHRASING
To the memory of Louis Zukofsky

1

clusteredtogether
squeezedtightly
literallycrampedforspace

a human condition

    humane or
hu may not

tea

& then again

the quali-
the levi-
the lucidi-

2

mental home
a state

strictly within my

proven   shall
(as if to encompass a shift in thot or tone)

meta-

physical
phorical

— man i did not know &

the beginning of
another story

3

the right hand side
the left hand side
the suicide

looking straight
a head

strictly a quest
shun good or evil?

two or
three lives

"one for yourself &
one more for the road"

4

head
thright

number &
number

brailing at the world

b lined like
a honeycomb

honey come home
com' 'ome
mmm

5

& drum corps

arrives

whistling in the dark
do do
      that's it you've got it

6
  6
    6

ORDINARY MAN

Bowed bass & piano (see bottom note bridge)

April/77

I'm just an or-di-na-ry man [Ho-hum] And I do things ordi-
na-rily as I can [Ho-hum] There is nothing extra-ordi-nary
I'm just an ordi-nary man And it's an or-di-na-ry day [Ho-hum]
And I do things in an ordi-na-ry way [Ho-hum] There is
nothing extra-or-di-nary This is an ordinary day [Ho-hum]
People say that Freud and Einstein opened people's eyes
People just don't re-a-lize They were ordinary guys. And it's an
ordinary day [Ho-hum] And another ordi-nary bird flies by [Ho-hum] There is
nothing extra-ordin-ary It's just an ordinary [Ho-hum]
Mister Armstrong got ap-plause for walking on the moon

Even walking on the moon will be ordinar-y

soon. This is an ordinary song, [hum] ordi-na-ri-ly I

sing it all day long. [hum] There is nothing extra-

or-di-nary. This is my ordinary song.

Sky This is an ordinary song Ordinarily I

Sing it all day long There is nothing extra

or-di-nary. This is my ordinary song.

* Lead in under Mike's humming

AUSTRALOPITHECUS

April 77

Aus-tra-lo-pith-e-cus. No longer with-a-cus. He went to heaven a long time a-go. Lovely Ne-and-ra-thol He was so wonder-ful. He went to heaven a long time a-go. All of the rel-a-tives of the family of man Back into history before history be-gan. They are all dead we're used to living a-lone So (1) how come my (2) And so dear mom & dad want me to stay home. How come my mother dear and mom & dad, I'm leaving home. How come my father dear Each time that I'm in love Do seem to re-ap-pear. Mother is very nice and Father is very nice, But I've lived with them long e-nough And I don't want to do it twice. And when I find a man it makes me so mad Because he

always starts to re- mind me of dad. Mother says I'm too young, Father
gives me a little kiss, And he calls me his daughter dear, that says I'll al-
ways be his. Now that I've grown up My respon-si- bil-i-ty
Is to the lives I've found and to be true to me.

The Vagina

1

I never had one.

2

I lived inside a woman for nine months & inside this male shell all of my life. I floated around on that side of the wall poking & kicking her not looking for exits till I needed them. There came a time I needed you vagina to get thru into this world. First thing I say at the light of day is 'waaah,' Ma.

3

I thot they all were hairless even tho I bathed with my mother I thot they all were like the little girl's who came naked to the door I delivered the paper to when I was nine even tho I read the typed porno stories my brother brought back from the navy when I was ten I thot they all were hairless like the nude women's in the sunbathing magazines in the pool hall in Port Arthur even tho I had to know different somewhere I thot they all were hairless & they weren't.

4

I always wanted one. I grew up wanting one. I thot cocks were okay but vaginas were really nifty. I liked that name for them because it began with 'v' and went 'g' in the middle. I never heard my mother or my sister mention them by name. They were an unspoken mouth & that was the mouth where real things were born. So I came out of that mouth with my mouth flapping 'waaah.' Oh I said that. I said that. I said 'waaah' Ma again & again after I was born.

5

When I was eleven this kid I knew took me to the drug-store where he worked & showed me some sanitary napkins for men. He said, 'you wear these when you get your period.' I remember he pointed the box out to me & it was way up in the back of this unlit top shelf. I figured I must have some kind of vestigial vagina which was bound to open. I waited almost two years. I never had one.

6

When sex happened I realized it was all a matter of muscles. I liked the way her muscles worked. She liked the way my muscle worked. It wasn't the one thing or the other thing but the way the two of them worked together. And that was where all the power & the feelings sprang from – the muscles. Alive alive oh.

7

Doorway. Frame. Mouth. Opening. Passage. The trick is to get from there to here thru her. Or the way Ellie misread that sign on the highway for years: RIGHT LANE MUST EXIST. And of course it's the old conundrum – the exit's the entrance. Exit Ma & I exist. And when I fell in love with Ellie I was entranced. Into a world. The world. This world. Our world. Worlds.

The Mouth

1

You were never supposed to talk when it was full. It was better to keep it shut if you had nothing to say. You were never supposed to shoot it off. It was better to be seen than heard. It got washed out with soap if you talked dirty. You were never supposed to mouth-off, give them any of your lip, turn up your nose at them, give them a dirty look, an evil eye or a baleful stare. So your mouth just sat there, in the middle of your still face, one more set of muscles trying not to give too much away. 'Hey! SMILE! what's the matter with you anyway?'

2

Probably there are all sorts of stories. Probably my mouth figures in all sorts of stories when I was little but I don't remember any of them. I don't remember any stories about my mouth but I remember it was there. I remember it was there and I talked & sang & ate & used it all the time. I don't remember anything about it but the mouth remembers. The mouth remembers what the brain can't quite wrap its tongue around & that's what my life's become. My life's become my mouth's remembering, telling stories with the brain's tongue.

3

I must have been nine. I'm pretty sure I was nine because I remember I was the new boy in school. I remember I was walking on my way there, the back way, thru the woods, & here was this kid walking towards me, George was his name, & I said 'hi George' & he said 'I don't like your mouth' & grabbed me & smashed my face into his knee. It was my first encounter with body art or it was my first encounter with someone else's idea of cosmetic surgery. It was translation or composition. He rearranged me.

4

The first dentist called me the Cavity Kid & put 35 fillings into me. The second dentist said the first dentist was a charlatan, that all the fillings had fallen out, & put 38 more fillings in me. The third dentist had the shakes from his years in the prisoner of war camp & called me his 'juicy one', saliva frothing from my mouth as his shaky hand approached me. The fourth dentist never looked at me. His nurse put me out with the sleeping gas & then he'd enter the room & fill me. The fifth dentist said my teeth were okay but my gums would have to go, he'd have to cut me. The sixth dentist said well he figured an operation on the foot was okay coz the foot was a long way away but the mouth was just a little close to where he thot he lived & boy did we ever agree because I'd begun to see that every time I thot of dentists I ended the sentence with the word 'me'. My mouth was me. I wasn't any ancient Egyptian who believed his Ka was in his nose – nosiree – I was just a Kanadian kid & had my heart in my mouth every time a dentist approached me.

5

It all begins with the mouth. I shouted waaa when I was born, maaa when I could name her, took her nipple in, the rubber nipple of the bottle later, the silver spoon, mashed peas, dirt, ants, anything with flavour I could shove there, took the tongue & flung it 'round the mouth making sounds, words, sentences, tried to say the things that made it possible to reach him, kiss her, get my tongue from my mouth into some other. I liked that, liked the fact the tongue could move in mouths other than its own, & that so many things began there – words did, meals, sex – & tho later you travelled down the body, below the belt, up there you could belt out a duet, share a belt of whiskey, undo your belts & put your mouths together. And I like the fact that we are rhymed, mouth to mouth, & that it begins here, on the tongue, in the pun, comes from mouth her mouth where we all come from.

6

I always said I was part of the oral tradition. I always said poetry was an oral art. When I went into therapy my therapist always said I had an oral personality. I got fixated on oral sex, oral gratification & notating the oral reality of the poem. At the age of five when Al Watts Jr was still my friend I actually said, when asked who could do something or other, 'me or Al' & only years later realized how the truth's flung out of you at certain points & runs on ahead. And here I've been for years running after me, trying to catch up, shouting 'it's the oral', 'it all depends on the oral', everybody looking at my bibliography, the too many books & pamphlets, saying with painful accuracy: 'that bp – he really runs off at the mouth.'

The Tonsils

I

They said 'you don't need them' but they were keen to cut them out. They said 'if they swell up they'll choke you to death' so you learned they cut things off if they might swell up. There were two of them in their sacs & they hung there in your throat. They cut them off.

2

I didn't have them long enough to grow attached to them but they were attached to me. It was my first real lesson in having no choice. It was my only time ever in a hospital as a kid & I wasn't even sick. I wasn't even sick but I had the operation. I had the operation that I didn't want & I didn't say 'no' because there was no choice really. I had everybody who was bigger than me telling me this thing was going to happen & me crying a lot & them telling me it was good for me. It was my first real lesson in having no attachments.

3

Almost everyone I knew had their tonsils out. Almost everyone I knew was told 'it's good for you.' Even tho none of us who had our tonsils out ever knew any kid who choked to death from having them in, almost everyone we knew had their tonsils out.

4

I miss my tonsils. I think my throat used to feel fuller. Now my throat feels empty a lot & maybe that's why I eat too fast filling the throat with as much as I can. Except food is no substitute for tonsils. The throat just gets empty again.

5

I was told I didn't need my tonsils. Maybe this is the way it is. Maybe as you grow older they tell you there are other bits you don't need & they cut them out. Maybe they just like cutting them out. Maybe tonsils are a delicacy doctors eat & the younger they are the sweeter. Maybe this is just paranoia. I bet if I had a lobotomy they could cut this paranoia out.

6

What cutting remarks! What rapier wit! What telling thrusts! Ah cut it out! Cut it short! He can't cut it! You said a mouthful!

7

There are two of them & they hang there in your throat. There are two of them in sacs & they swell up. Now there are none. Gosh these words seem empty!

The Chest

1

You were obsessed with it. Everyone was obsessed with it. On the edge of thirteen when Carol Wisdom's chest started to develop you couldn't take your eyes off it. Until you were twelve everyone who was your age had a chest. But then you turned thirteen & you had a chest & she had breasts on her chest & your chest was puny & he really had a chest & she was chesty & all the bad puns began about being 'chest friends' & it was 'chest too much' or 'two much' or 'two for tea anytime baby' (which of course you always said to a guy coz you were too embarrassed to say it to a girl) & suddenly you had discovered chests as if they had never been there before & they were everywhere, everywhere, & you were obsessed with them.

2

From the age of five to the age of sixteen you kept getting chest colds. Once a year for three weeks you'd be sick in bed, your voice getting deeper (which you liked), your breathing shallower (which you hated), your nostrils redder, your face whiter, saying mutter for mother muttering for her. She'd bring you gingerale (to soothe your throat), vicks vaporub (to clear your head), & you'd say 'I'm gedding bedder' over & over again like a charm clutched to your hopeless chest, 'I'm gedding bedder' you'd say, sinking further into the sheets, 'I'm gedding bedder', til the bed & you were one pale continuous tone, white on white in white, 'I'm gedding bedder – bedder.'

3

It was where longing resided. It was what you played your cards close to. It was one of the few body parts rhymed with the furniture & it held hope or tea or linen. It was a clear noun, substantial, the only named part that didn't seem small, didn't seem somehow smaller thru naming. It had no funny names or corny names or dirty names & it was the largest part of all. You stuck it out. You puffed it up. It was chest. What it was was chest.

4

You didn't think of the chest as sensitive until you danced with her. You were thirteen & the dance floor was crowded & tho the moving bodies of your friends pressed you together you would only allow your chests to touch & there was heat & pressure & movement between you & your chest was ten times more sensitive than your hands, felt more than your eyes could see, & your trapped heart pounded as if you would die, explode, right there before her eyes, disintegrate from the ache & longing. You were in love, your chests were in love, as the music & the crowd carried you, pressing you closer & closer together, over that moving dance floor that dark warm August night.

When you went into therapy all the language changed. Now the chest was something you got things off of or bared, some place you shouldn't keep things inside of, as if it were a vessel & feelings held there grew stagnant, festered, expanded under pressure until released to air. In the shaky diagramming of the unconscious it was where deep lay — deep feelings, deep disturbance — or you thot it was because weren't you always being told you shouldn't be too heady, shouldn't talk off the top of your head, that it was bad to be cut off at the neck, dead from the neck down, & from the neck down is where the chest is. But not too far down because after all you weren't supposed to dump shit on anyone either, or talk a load of crap, piss on them, be a shit, & what was left then but the chest unless, of course, you had a gut feeling. But gut was too ambiguous, too subject to the charge you were just spewing vomit. No. It was the chest. It had to be the chest; that was where the heart was & the heart was good. You were good-hearted, had a lot of heart &, when you got right down to things you had a heart to heart, really opened up, bared your chest & spoke from your heart all your real feelings, your deep feelings, got everything off your chest, just like you were supposed to.

The Lungs: A Draft

for Robert Kroetsch

I

This is a breath line. I said. This is a breathline. Line up, he said. Suck your stomach in Nichol, I don't want to see you breathe. I didn't breathe. This was a no breath line. He said. Six or eight or ten of us not breathing while he walked down the line, holding our breath while he looked us over, while he chose one of us to punch in the gut, to see how tough our stomach muscles were he said, stomachs pulled in, lungs pushed out, waiting while he paced back and forth, while he paused in front of each of us and then moved on, this small smile playing across his lips. Waiting. A breathless line. I said.

2

I was staying at Bob and Smaro's place in Winnipeg. I was sleeping on the floor in Smaro's study. I was getting up early in the morning, like I tend to do, getting up early and going into the livingroom. I was sitting down in a chair and reading a copy of a new book on literary theory or literary criticism Smaro had brought back from some recent trip as she tends to do. I was just turning the page, just beginning to get into the book when Bob appeared at the top of the stairs, when Bob came down the stairs from the upper floor, not really awake, came down the stairs anyway, Bob, muttering to himself, 'life, the great tyrant that makes you go on breathing.' And I thought about breathing. I thought about life. I thought about those great tyrants the lungs, about the lung poems I've tried to perfect in various ways, the lung poems Bob's written, written about, lung forms. And I thought about the lungs sitting there, inside the chest – inhaling – exhaling. And I thought to myself, to myself because Bob was in no mood to hear it, I thought 'life's about going the lung distance.' Just that. And it is.

3

We were maybe five, Al Watts Jr and me, no more than five, and we had snuck out back, behind the garage, to try a smoke. It was just the way you read it in all those nostalgic memoirs of male childhood. It was authentic. It was a prairie day in Winnipeg in the late 40's and there we were, two buddies sharing a furtive puff on a stolen cigarette. And just like in all the other stories the father showed up, Al Watts Sr, suddenly appeared around the corner of the garage and said 'so you boys want to smoke, eh?' If only we'd read the stories. If only we'd had the stories read to us. We'd have known then how the whole thing had to end, we'd have known what part the dad plays in these kinds of tales. But we hadn't. We didn't. We said yes we really did want to smoke. And we did. Al Watts Sr took us home, took us back to his study, the room he very seldom took us into, and opened up his box of cigars and offered one to each of us. We should have known. We really should have known when he lit them for us and told us to really suck in, to take that smoke right down into our lungs, we should have known what was coming. We didn't. We did it just the way he said. We sucked that smoke right in, right down to our lungs, and of course we started hacking, of course we started coughing, trying to fling the cigars away. But he made us take another smoke, he made us take another three or four good drags on the cigar, until our bodies were racked from the coughing, until our lungs ached from the lunge and heave of trying to push the smoke out. And we didn't want to smoke anymore, I didn't want to smoke anymore, I never really wanted to touch a cigarette again. Even when I was a teenager and hanging out with Easter Egg on his old scow down in Coal Harbour and he'd offer me a toke, I never could take the smoke into my lungs again. Except that after I turned 30 I started smoking cigars. And even though I didn't take the smoke into my lungs, even though I just held it there in the mouth and let it go, when I thought about it it really didn't make much sense. It didn't you know. Look what had happened to me with Al Watts Sr and Al Watts Jr those many many years ago. This wasn't supposed to be the outcome. This wasn't supposed to be the way the story goes.

But it was as if the lungs wanted me to do it. As if the lungs had a memory all their own and I was forced to relive it. Not a primal scream but a primal puff, primal smoke from a primal prairie fire. As if the whole childhood episode had been like one of those moral tales where the reader takes a different lesson from the one the writer intended. Or like one of those shaggy dog jokes, where the punch line comes way after the joke should have ended, way after the person listening has lost all interest in what's being said. Lung time. Different from the head's.

4

When do you first think of your lungs? When you're young and tiny and turning blue and you can't get your breath because something is happening to you like my mom told me it happened to me? When you're five and choking over your first smoke like I just told you? When you start to sing in the choir and the choirmaster tells you to really fill your lungs with air, your stomach, and support the sound from down there, inside the body? When you take up running, gasp for that last breath hoping to bring the tape nearer, the finish line, hoping the lungs will hold for the final lunge? Do you think of them then? In a moment like this, trying to remember, can you even say 'I remember *this* about my lungs'? No. No. Almost no memories at all. Only the notion that they're there pumping away, just beneath the surface of these lines, however much these lines do or don't acknowledge them. One of those parts you can't do without. Two of them. 'The bellows,' he bellows, airing his opinion. Because to air is human. To forgive the divine. Bellowing our prays, our songs. Bellowing our lung-ings.

A draft he calls it. Like it blew in through a crack in the mind. Just a bunch of hot air. As when you're really hot, get the cadences to fall, the syllables to trot past the eye and ear just the way you see and hear them in the mind. As tho the mind tapped the lung and each thot hung there in its proper place. 'It's just a draft. I'll get it right later.' He feels the breath heave. He hears the words start as the heart pumps and the lungs take all that air and squeeze it in there, into the blood stream flows thru the mind. No next time when the lungs stop. Like that last sentence on the tongue, hangs in the air after the lungs have pressed their last square inch of it out in the absolute moment of death, only the body left: 'I'll get it right next time.'

The Fingers

for Mary Griffin

I

There were ten of them. Or were there eight? Everyone always said the thumbs were different. They made you human. They let you know you weren't a great ape. Even tho his sister told him they'd found him in the zoo, a forlorn hairless little monkey the other monkeys had rejected, that ma had taken pity on him and brought him home with them, he knew he was human. He flexed his eight fingers and his two thumbs and knew he was human. Even when the three year old from next door his sister had taught to call him 'monkey' came in and called him 'monkey' in front of all those guests at the dinner table, he knew. He flexed his fingers. He twiddled his thumbs. 'I'm human,' he said and he knew.

2

In all the early photos he is holding his sister's hand, his fingers wrapped around her fingers, grabbing hold, hanging on. He is doing this in photo after photo, the left hand usually, the left fingers, while the right hand hangs at his side or pushes his brother away as his brother attempts to hold his hand, pushes his brother away with his right fingers while his left fingers curl ever more tightly around his sister's. And these are his write fingers too, grasping the pen he uses to describe this as he stares at the fingers of his left hand, open now and empty, his sister hundreds of miles away, his right fingers wrapped around this pen, grabbing hold, hanging on, full of these descriptions, while his left hand hangs at his side.

3

'Take his hand,' they'd say, 'c'mon give him a hand.' 'It's very handy,' they'd add, by way of explanation, 'when the kids lend a hand, very touching,' they'd say, touching their eyes with their handkerchiefs. And if he couldn't grasp what they were saying, couldn't handle it, they'd put their fingers to their heads drawing circles with their fingertips, touch their fingers to their brows tapping them, as tho they were giving him the mental finger, as tho they were fingering him as mental. And everywhere he turned there were fingers: pointed at him as they shouted 'bang bang you're dead'; raised to ask questions, raised to answer them; stuck out to signal this or that turn. Fingers like sharks as they wagged their jaws at him. Fins. GRRR.

4

They put him in the front line in the touch football game. They put him in the front line in front of Moose. They put him in front of Moose whom noone else would stand in front of. They put him in the front line where he'd lean forward, balancing on his fingertips, as the Quarterback called the signals, as the ball was snapped, as Moose trampled over him rushing to follow the ball in. They put him in the front line and Moose trampled over him again and again, game after game, until the day his finger broke, snapped as he tried to touch Moose, as he tried to lay a hand on him, tried to carry out, somehow, the rules of the game. He wore a cast for weeks, covering his wrist and snaking out along his broken finger like a hook and when they asked what had happened, how had he broken his finger, he told them 'playing touch football'. And nobody laughed because nobody else would get in line in front of Moose. Noone else could or would touch him.

5

The thing was he couldn't control his fingers properly. First there was the writing, making the O's so large they travelled above and below the blue lines in his copy book, beyond the red margin to the left of his pen. And he was told to get more control so he learned to hold the pen funny, gripping it with three fingers as it rested on a fourth. And he learned to write small and tiny, learned to write between the lines, to leave so much white space around the writing that noone could read it. And they wanted him to write larger again and he couldn't. He could contain the fingers but he couldn't control them. Like later with the model plane kits – balsa wood, plastic – trying to make the bits fit, trying to be so careful, so precise, and he couldn't, wasn't, his fingers kept fumbling things, snapping them, clumsy in the attempt to apply decals, paint, glue, and he would finish these models, hold them up on his fingertips simulating flight, but they wouldn't, didn't, looked like they never had, never would, fly. They just sat there, on his fingers, on his shelf, making him feel guilty, useless, as if they were pointing the finger at him, at his failure, his inability to control his fingers.

6

This is the way it went. He was to keep his sticky fingers off the dining room table. He was to keep his fingers to himself. He was not to finger himself (which made his fingers sticky), or her (which made his fingers sticky), or stick his finger in his nose (which made his fingers sticky). He was to keep them out of the cookie jar, off of the pie, on the handlebars, inside the car, around the golf club, above the table. But he was supposed to get a grip on himself, get a good grasp of languages, problems, situations, a good grasp on reality, be able to reach people, touch them, get a feel for them, put his finger on the solution almost instantly. And you have to hand it to him, he handled the whole thing like a five finger exercise, kept his fingers on the pulse of the notion even when his reach exceeded his grasp, even when he was losing his grip, even when his head was whirling with more conflicting messages than you could count on the fingers of both hands, he handled them, he kept them in hand.

7

First he was always trying to control his fingers. Later he learned the fingers controlled everything. Everyone thot in tens and had ten fingers (sort of) and when push came to shove anyone of them might be the one to push the big red button. Early on he learned the fingers gave you pleasure. You could feed yourself, play with yourself, finger things out, as you had to. Later he learned his fingers could give other people pleasure too, other fingers could give him pleasure, in the reaching, touching, evenhandedness of love. And when she married him, he took the ring that they had bought and placed it on her finger. And he cried. And she cried. And now he knew that finger had a real ring to it, there was something there, and maybe this was the first step in beginning to grasp it.

8

What he wanted to do was play a musical instrument so he took up the violin. He took up the violin because they had one at school noone else wanted to play and they offered it to him, a real hand-me-down, offered him lessons and the violin and he went for it, got his hands on it and off he went. Except everyone at home hated it when he played it, hated it because he couldn't get the fingering right no matter how hard he tried, stood in the other room their fingers in their ringing ears as his fingers tried to wring the right sounds from the strings. And he couldn't, he didn't, he never will make that violin sing. Because he was all thumbs. Because his hands went haywire. Because his fingers fumbled it, his digits, dig it, didn't.

9

After he had been writing for awhile he became aware of how many times he used the word 'fingers', the fact of them, the image of them, in his poems. All that talk of reaching and touching, all those barriers his fingers seemed to encounter between him and some imagined other. The metaphors. The similes. The symbolisms. And then one day he realized that of course he was always staring at his hand when he wrote, was always watching the pen as it moved along, gripped by his fingers, his fingers floating there in front of his eyes just above the words, above that single white sheet, just above these words i'm writing now, his fingers between him and all that, like another person, a third

88

person, when all along you thot it was just the two of you talking and he suddenly realized it was the three of them, handing it on from one to the other, his hand translating itself, his words slipping thru his fingers into the written world. You.

10

Much later he began to write for puppets and there he was, day after day, watching his words come out of the mouths of fingers, watching hands turn to each other and say the lines he had spent so long struggling to perfect. And one day one of the hands turned to him and said: 'Hey, bp, what do you think?' And it had always been his fingers talking, his fingers shaping the letters, the words, that funny grip around the pen, the language, and he lifted his hand up, opening and closing his fingers, and said: 'Nothing.'

The Hips

1

Not hip.

2

Maw called them 'the Workman hips.' 'Too bad,' she'd say to me, 'you've got the Workman hips. Too bad,' she'd say to my sister, 'you've got the Workman hips. Too bad,' she'd say to my nieces, shaking her head in dismay, 'you've got the Workman hips,' she'd say, as generation after generation of family swayed past her on their way into history, 'you've got the Workman hips. Too bad,' she'd say.

3

We tend not to think of them as different. We tend not to think of them as unique. We refer to them by direction – left or right – and when they're really wide we say 'hey, what a caboose,' as the hips sway away, left, then right, then left, disappearing in the distance. We tend to think of them distantly, something that's there where the body gets interesting, interested, and tho we say 'nice pair of hips,' it's usually the waist, the way the bum shapes itself, the belly, crotch, we're referring to. But then one day someone places their hand on your hip, lovingly, expectantly, and the hip they touch is different, unique, left or right, and it carries you away as they lay their hand there and you let it stay. You place your hand on their hip, press your bodies close together and say okay. Let the hips carry you away.

4

I was just a kid. We were living in Port Arthur and it was Saturday afternoon and I had nothing else to do so I rode my bike down Oliver Road towards downtown and there was this big crowd gathered in an open field near a lumber yard and tables had been set up made of saw horses and spare lumber where you could buy juice and pop and there were booths with people in them selling things and people standing outside them buying things and I rode my bicycle into that field under the fluttering banners someone had strung around it and there was a woman standing there in the middle of the crowd who had the biggest hips I'd ever seen. It turned out her name was Boxcar Annie or, at least, that's what the announcer said as I got off my bike, he said that we were about to see a log-chopping contest and Boxcar Annie, who was also called the Queen of the Hoboes and must've weighed at least 300 pounds, was the lone woman contestant. The idea was that each contestant had to chop a log clean thru and whoever finished first was the winner and he told them all to wait until he yelled go and he yelled go and I watched the whole contest, sweating man after burly sweating man and, of course, Boxcar Annie, who had the biggest hips I'd ever seen and will ever see, and Boxcar Annie beat every man in the place, beat them all easily, and everyone cheered and said how terrific Annie was, she really was the Queen of the Hoboes, and afterwards Annie went off to drink beer with the men she'd beaten and I got back on my bike and rode it all the way back up the hill to home. And I never have forgotten the sight of her, the way she chopped wood so effortlessly, precisely, rhythmically, chips flying, hips swaying, the biggest hips I've ever ever seen.

5

It was because of my hips I started writing. I was in Grade 4. It was late fall or early spring, I can't remember which, but I remember the ditch, the one near the school, and it was full of icy slush and a friend dared me to jump across it so I did. I remember leaping through the air and barely making it halfway across before my left foot, which was pointed down, began to enter the thick icy mixture of slush and water, my right leg still vainly reaching towards the far side of the ditch as my left leg followed my left foot down towards the untouched bottom, and I landed like some bad imitation of a ballet dancer, struck, my left leg burying itself in that slush right up to my hip, stuck, my right leg floating on the top. My hips kept me afloat. Or at least that's what the firemen said to my Maw when they brought me home after rescuing me. I'd been stuck in that freezing sludge for over an hour while my friend ran and told the teacher who phoned the fire department who came and laid ladders across on either side of me and pulled me up and out, and the firemen said that that ditch was so deep and the sludge so like quicksand I would've drowned if it hadn't been for the

strange position of my legs and hips. And the cold I caught
from bring stuck in the ditch turned into bronchitis and
they kept me home from school for over two weeks and
during that time I wrote my first novel, *The Sailor From
Mars,* all 26 chapters written by hand in a school copy book.
It was all about a Martian sailor who came to Earth, went to
work on a sailing ship and, along the way, fell in love with a
girl called Luna who, I remember writing, 'was not of this
world.' I can't remember now how the novel ended, or even
how it went, and my Maw threw it away by mistake three
years later so there's no way I can go back and refresh my
memory, but I do remember that when I went back to
school I showed it to my teacher and she read the whole
thing to the class, a bit every morning for a week or two, just
like a real serial, the kind I used to listen to all the time on the
radio, and she said she liked it, and the kids said they liked it,
and of course I loved it. I was alive and now I was a writer
too. And really, when you get right down to it, you have to
admit it was all thanks to my hips. And whenever people ask
me 'how did you become a writer,' I always tend to say 'I just
fell into it.' Right up to my hips. Believe me.

6

Hip hip hooray, they'd say. Two hips, hooray? There had
to be some meaning in it somewhere, some symbolism. Hip
hip hooray, hip hip hooray, which meant someone had done
something, outstanding, unique even, was okay. But later,
when I was sixteen and in Grade 13 at King Eddy in Van-
couver, I joined the Jazz Club and began to hang around
jazz clubs with Sandy, whose brother was a jazz musician.
And in all those clubs I went to – The Black Spot, Java Jazz,
clubs that came and went and I can no longer attach a name
to – in all those clubs I went to I learned it was not hip to
shout hooray. It was not even hip to double the hip. It was
only hip to be hip, single, unique, that was okay. So we sat

there and said nothing except 'yeah' or 'hey' when the band was great, when the soloist was transported away in an improvisation we nodded, maybe grinned, tho even grinning was suspect in those days. Hip. Just hip. No hooray.

7

You can never forget about your hips. My Maw was always aware of her hips. She'd put on a dress and turn and look at herself in the mirror and sigh and you knew she was sighing about her hips. And even when they were invisible, like the time my Maw was in the hospital, the sheet pulled up to her waist, and the nurse came in and said 'my aren't you petite,' my Maw couldn't resist saying 'wait until you pull down this sheet,' because she couldn't forget about her hips. And now most days I feel this pain in my left hip, if I sit in a chair that isn't made just right, I feel this pain in my left hip, and I think about Maw, I think about Grandmaw, I wonder if all their lives too there was this nagging little pain saying I won't let you forget about me. And you don't let me forget about you do you? You're there reminding me, every time I stand too long, reminding me, every time the chair's too soft or too hard or too wrong. You're never going to let me forget about you. Are you hip?

The Anus

I

It is an us – & yes we all have them. And as far as I can tell I never was able to see much difference between them. Just that little pucker among the cheeks. Whistle.

2

My mother stuck a tube up it to give me an enema. I remember it was good for what ailed me. I remember it really cleaned me out. I remember lying over her knees with my pants down & her sticking this tube up me & me screaming 'THAT'S ENOUGH!' I remember thinking ma was the enema and the anus us. That's what confuse us say. Confuse us say an us don't make we we.

3

We talked about it more than anything else down there. We didn't so much name it as allude to it. My maw said 'wherever you be may your winds blow free' or 'fox smells its own hole first.' My maw said 'whoever makes a smell like that must be rotten inside.' It was one of the big connections with the inside & thru it she knew whether you were sick or healthy & whether or not you needed an enema. You always looked to see if the things that came from it were firm or messy. You never referred to where they came from except to say the bum & to wonder, really, whether you had wiped it.

4

When I read my first porno comic I found the word poot. People would be making love & fart & the sound effect read poot, poot, poot. Just the way the little engine that could said toot, toot, toot. Just like the joke about the fireman's big red fire engine going in & out of his wife's firehall. Hoot, hoot. Oot. I was trying to figure it oot.

5

I came out of the movie with some friends & there was a christian recruiting group singing hymns across the street & this car drove by with this guy's ass stuck out the window hanging a moon for the world to see & the choir kept on singing just a closer walk with thee.

6

The bum isn't the anus. The moon isn't green cheese. The last rose of summer is impossible to determine but when he drops it you know he's been there. Like my one brother hung a moon over my other brother's sleeping face. Then he dropped a rose that smelled like green cheese & my brother woke up yelling 'get your bum out of my face!'

7

I just thot 'there's too many rymes in this piece.' I just thot 'the anus rymes both men & women.' I just thot about this guy I knew who after another guy raped him said 'he used me like a woman' & the woman I knew who objecting to her lover's advances said 'he wanted to use me like a man.' I just thot about the anus & wrote down all I could. I just thot that the way I should end this piece is with the word 'anus' coz that's where a certain process in the body ends. I just thot that & now here I am writing this sentence's anus.

The Toes

I

I was lying on my back on the grass in the park in front of our house staring at them & thot how ugly they looked. I was fifteen & really depressed & the clouds blew over the park & I stared at these two great clubs of flesh & bone with five little stubs sticking out of each of them & thot how ugly they looked & how maybe I should kill myself. I lay in the long grass beneath the oak trees & thot about killing myself & the ugliness of my toes & decided my suicide would have to be because of something else. This was the first time I ever really looked at my toes & boy were they something else. They were ugly.

2

In Port Arthur we went to the shoe section in the big department store where they had the free X-ray machine & shoved our feet into it & stared into the viewer & saw the bones in our toes moving. It was like the peepshow movieola we looked into at the sideshow where we always ran out of quarters just before we got to see the woman with all her clothes off but we saw our toes with all their flesh off & there were ten sets of bones we wiggled & there was no lead shielding & we did it almost every weekend for months. Maybe they mutated. Maybe they looked so ugly later because they'd mutated & it's all the fault of the shoe department in the big store whose name I no longer remember so there's nobody I can sue. Maybe this is the clue. Maybe postmodern writers like me all have post-atomic poetic feet & that's what makes them ugly to the pre-atomic eye & difficult to notate. Maybe this is THE ATTACK OF THE MUTANT POST-ATOMIC FEET! Maybe this is why we're always saying the words: 'take me to your reader.'

3

It was okay to talk about feet. It was okay to talk about toes. It was never okay to talk about toe-jam. If you talked about toe-jam you were really gross. I've never even seen the word spelt before. I think I like it best just the way I've spelt it here, with the hyphen between the two words 'toe' & 'jam,' like the dark grungy hyphen you were embarrassed to discover there, between your toes, inside your sock, your shoe, where you were never able to figure how the toe-jam got.

4

When Ellie & I moved in together we bought a house with six other people on Warren Road & the next door neighbours had a dog named 'toes.' It was like a sick joke & I felt fifteen again & the stupid dog chased me every time I walked from the house to the coach house & back again. It was like a bad dream where the repressed returns & there I was, toes yapping at me, toes jumping at me, toes trying to step on me, ugly & depressing & out to get me.

5

I forget when I first noticed my toenails grew funny. Probably the same day I realized my feet were ugly. The big toenails were worst of all, flaky & fragmented, & the little toenails, almost non-existent, & the ones in between curling around the stubs of the toes, hugging them, so that even now, except for the big toe (which gets sharp & jagged & rips my socks), I don't have to cut them for months unless, of course, I feel like it. But it is easier if you keep them cut because of the dirt that wedges under them. And toenails are dull, like this paragraph, & in writing we're warned to cut the dull short. Except that no matter how short I cut them they're still dull & lately I began to think that maybe all you are saying when you say 'it's dull' is 'it's ugly & difficult to control'. And it really struck me the way the toenails curl around pressed flat against the stubby pink surfaces of the toes as tho they were hiding from me, fighting for their lives, feeding on the dirt & jam accumulated there, in the dark of the shoe, growing.

6

Why were toes 'piggies?' Why did one of them go to market? When that last little piggie went 'wee-wee-wee,' how come he did it all the way home? We all know pigs become sausages & sausages look just like toes. Where do these metaphors & similes, these symbolisms, come from? Who makes up these resemblances, these languages, anyway? Why is it some days the words look so strange, so other, almost as if someone somewhere's speaking to me from behind them, thru them, trying to make me understand, instruct me, maybe even warn me – you know, trying to keep me on my toes?

Sum of the Parts

I

So many things inside me I am not in touch with. So many things I depend on that I never see, pray I never see. As in the horror movie when the monster's taloned hand reaches in and pulls out your living spleen. So many things with such strange names. The sound of them is enough to make me vomit. And when I do, well, there it is, something from inside me, and I am in touch with it, can smell it, taste it, feel it, praying I'll never have to again, praying it will stop, the contraction in the throat, the sound from beyond the tongue, more in touch with my insides than I really wanted.

2

If you're unlucky you get to meet them. If you're lucky you never get to meet them at all, they just nestle there, inside your body, monitoring, processing, producing, while you go about your life, oblivious. And this is the real organ music, the harmony of these spheres, the way the different organs play together, work, at that level beyond consciousness of which all consciousness is composed, the real unconscious, the unseen.

3

It's the old problem of writing about something you know nothing about. I can do the research, read the books, but it's not the same. It's not the same. Tho they name the organs and the names are the same they're not the same organs as the organs sitting here inside me – the bpNichol liver, the bpNichol kidney, the bladder, pancreas, b p – Collected workings I think of as me. Which is why I worry if the doctor knows me, my work, when I go in, worry that that doctor may be a *real* collector, a completist. So you never ever say to the doctor, 'Doctor, please save me.' No, you never say that. You say, 'what's wrong with me?' or 'I'm in rotten shape!' or, even better, 'I'm worthless!', downplaying yourself, devaluing yourself, making yourself as miserable and undesirable as possible till the doctor says, 'Collect yourself!' And you do. And he doesn't. Which is how you want things to be.

4

I almost got to meet my thyroid. I had been to see the Doctor and the Doctor said well it looked like my thyroid was enlarged and really I should get a thyroid scan and before you could say goiter there I was in this tiny room strapped down under this big machine & the technician was saying not to worry because nothing bad was going to happen, I only had to lie there as still as possible for fifteen minutes or so and then I could get up and leave. So I lay there, as still as possible, thinking about my thyroid, thinking about leaving, my nose itching, my throat dry, lay there aware of my thyroid, tho I couldn't see it, even tho I couldn't see the technician who even then was looking at it, pictures of it, aware of my unseen thyroid, aware of the unseen technician who had so carefully left the room after she had strapped me down under the big machine, who had so carefully closed the lead-shielded doors and told me not to worry. And of course I worried. I always worry. Even tho you say you'd like to see it, you always worry when there's a chance you might finally get your wish, might finally see *it*, the unseen, might finally enter into that world, like turning inside out, a raw feeling. See? No, you don't want to see.

5

After I threw my back out I had more X-Rays, X-Rays of the lumbar sacrum region. Only the Doctor that day was giving a lecture to these two trainees and as the technician shoved me around on the cold steel table he would whisper his commentaries. It was like those old TV game shows where the announcer would say 'what the studio audience doesn't know is,' and the trouble was I didn't know you see. You live your whole life making do with only the reflection of certain parts, making do with simply the names of your inner organs, their descriptions in books, while all around you are people who may actually have seen them, know directly what you only glimpse third-hand. Like your back. Every stranger on the street has had the chance to look at it but you only know it thru mirrors, photographs that other people take of you. And there are Doctors and Nurses who have cut you open, watched your blood flow, seen your heart pulse, know the inner man or woman. And these aren't just metaphors you know these aren't just similes. It is a discipline. We learn to see with the third eye, to listen with the third ear, to touch the unknown with the third hand, to walk down dark streets in search of the hidden, the unseen, while in the air around us invisible presences pick up their zithers and begin to play the Third Man Theme.

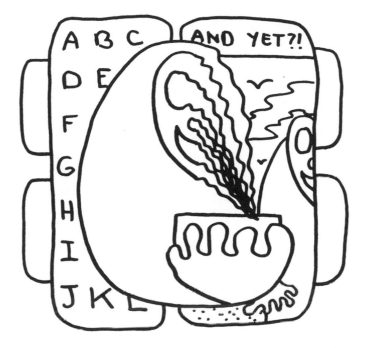

Allegory #7

the circumference of the spoken word

any word is made up of a sequence of lip movements during which the word is sounded.

example:

W   OR   D

thus (if we are to take the title of this particular system literally) the circumference of "word" as it is spoken would be the total of the circumference of each lip opening during its speaking.

the circumference of "w" + the circumference of "or" + the circumference of "d" = the circumference of "word"

we can propose then a formula which would give us the circumference of any spoken word.

$$W = C_1 + C_2 + C_3 \text{ etc}$$

where W is the circumference of any word, C the circumference of the mouth opening at the apex of its particular phonemic movement & where 1,2,3 etc indicates the particular phoneme in terms of its place in the relevant speech sequence.

commentary:

immediately upon completing the first draft of this system, which i had tentatively titled THE CIR-CUMFERENCE OF THE WORD, i realized the necessity for the more accurate titling which now accompanies it because of two elements: 1) ventriloquism & 2) printed language. these two elements gave rise to two subsequent systems: PROBABLE SYSTEMS 21, the weight of speech (for Rube Goldberg) & PROBABLE SYSTEMS 24, physical contexts of human speech. it is worth pointing out tho that this system is hopelessly inadequate because of the variables present in any group of human speakers. the best one could hope for is a broad enough sampling to enable us to arrive at a statistical approximation of what the circumference of a particular word would be.

CCMC WITH STEVE MCCAFFERY (SKETCHING 2)

1

an empty stage

a place in which there is nothing
there are objects

no objections

a beginning

2

birds

this is an abstraction

this is traction when
the finger slips
tips

mouth music muses

chooses
                which is not a ryme

time's abandoned for a tone
a kind of random tune
moves the meant

3

saxophony

symphony

synthesizerphony

guitaphony

"do the pony phony"

4

screaming or a kind of pleading

is there a value
judgement is there

simply speaking simply

chordial
musical

broad way

5

voices / ices / o
ver
    / er
        /
            hmmm

an observation in the midst of
not / sing / ing

"in the human head"

walking the bass line

/ home /

6

two beats

two drums

two cheeks
pounded

im

      er again

WILLED

7

auto horn
auto harp
auto heart

YELLING

siren
sighing wren
weep willed

BIRDLAND

8

quarreltet

argumental

so the brain in brain is
mainly in the plain telling

or a sea
washes over me

sound wave

9

altoed states

his attack jack is back to basics
cohere to there

to & fro in the world &
struck sure

flim flamenco densities

u's
   v's

y z

H (AN ALPHHABET)

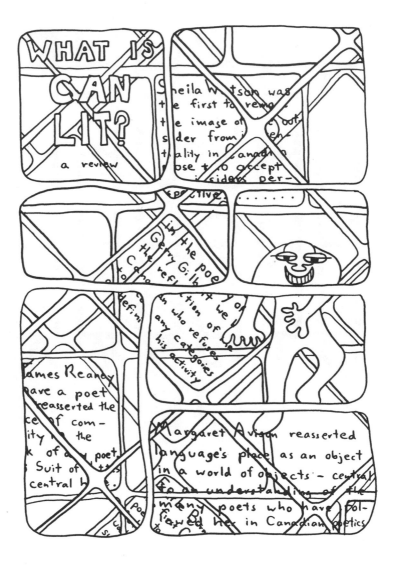

III

LETTERS FROM A RAINY SEASON

I

the circle
is of faces
looking inwards
                    towards
the centre
            of
the table

the table
at which
caught back
in the brain's shell

in the tongue's prison
till
my lips
crumble

            the
knuckles of my hands
burst forth in
raw air

the circle
turns
around me

faces
surround me
contorted as
my own

2

seated round
we hear
the sound
of feet
     across
the ceiling, the floor
of someone's room
somewhere
in this house

whose son, whose daughter
moves there, above us, moves
in the upper reaches
of our air

where
     do
the walls
       end
their movements
in doors

where
     do
the windows
       frame
· their world

where
     do
my own
     windows
       move

that they appear   here
to frame
my eyes

am i
forever to see
even here
at this table
the image
of the sea?

and they
who move above us
what do
they
      see?

3
beyond
the eye

taken

all
that i can see

hear

broken down
for you

offered

insight
in-

side
a circling

movement

that
surrounds us

sitting

backs to
the door

the eye
turns toward

4
now the sea
brings in
its changes

the bells
sundays
ring

a strangeness
takes the heart
to windows

air   air

wherever
the sea moves

wherever

the sun
shines
or reaches

the eyes
follow
following

from the chair
seated
watching

the boats
move
ringing

the changes
the finger
traces

to bring
the strangeness
thru

5

the sun
the breast
the eye

that which
gives, that which
takes, that which

yields
is given to
and gives

that which
surrounds, that which
enfolds, that which

opens
is opened to
in opening

that which
is spoken of
and speaks

its name
upon our breath
in various guises

6

such
        care
was taken
            to
board
        it
up
    that
even after all these years
removing the nails
was difficult

inside
the dank smell
of rot
            dead leaves
floorboards
to fall thru

            that
someone
            had
lived here
was obvious
                only
by
the planks
over the windows

— a whole winter
                    to
fix
    the place up

it seemed
a plague,
a season
          of rains,
had struck us
left us
in the middle
of wreckage

              we
stripped it bare
(the circular
living room, the hall) where
they'd painted over
the natural wood
we scraped it clean

re-
built it — placed
ourselves there
with
what skill
we had

          the
former owner

says
      he
finds it
hard
      to believe

7

scrub &
the trees

the fox runs
towards the sea
from the burrow
in the hollow

a place
          by
the ocean

rain falling

where we sit
a view of
the lighthouse

each time
to venture out
seems daring

someone
we love
to wait

a reason
for returning

DAPHNE MARLATT + MICHAEL ONDAATJE caught
in relaxed mode while researching 3rd Inter-
national Indian Ocean Nostalgic Notation Meet.
Ondaatje won in the Novel Noun division while
Marlatt swept the Holding-the-Breath-Line-
Longest competition.   #5 in a series.

EASTER POME

```
    p u l p i t            t u l i p s
     p u l     p i t       t u l    i p s
    p u  l     p  i t    t u  l    i  p s
  p  u  l      p  i  t t  u  l     i  p  s
  p  u  l      p  t  i u t  l      i  p  s
  p  u  l      t  u  p l  i  t     i  p  s
  p  u  t      u  l  l i  p  i     t  p  s
  p  t  u      l  i  u p  l  p     i  t  s
  t  u  l      i  p  p s u  l      p  i  t
  t  u  l      i  p  s p u  l      p  i  t
   t u  l      i  p s    p u  l    p  i t
    t u l     i p s       p u l    p i t
     t u l i p s            p u l p i t
```

```
drum      anda      wheel
anda      drum      andaw
heel      anda      druma
ndaw      heel      andad
ruma      ndaw      heela
ndad      ruma      ndawh
eela      ndad      ruman
dawh      eela      ndadr
uman      dawh      eelan
dadr      uman      dawhe
elan      dadr      umand
awhe      elan      dadru
mand      awhe      eland
adru      mand      awhee
land      adru      manda
whee      land      adrum
anda      whee      landa
drum      anda      wheel
```

DREAM ANTHOLOGY 2
(From Sheila Watson's *Six Questions After Michael Anthin*)

I start out with the idea of place to fix you there Mommy.
Interwoven – interspecies. .

in the dream Sheila offers to read to me from a new story she
has written called *BEAR* after the character of Kallisto in
her story *ANTIGONE*. she tells me she has already read it
to Daphne Marlatt & Maureen Jennings. but before that she
proposes to read to me from a little piece she has written
called *SIX QUESTIONS AFTER MICHAEL ANTHIN* ,
in order to show me how she is using language to hinge
from reference to reference in a dream oriented way. she
cites as an example the shift from *Georgina* to *garage* in which
the buried associative hinge is *Gene's garage* which is near
where she lives. she starts to read to me as above from a
hand-written notebook & then stops & says "no, this is an
earlier draft. i'll read to you from the latest draft", and begins
to look for it.

associatively the day before i had been having a long talk
with Michael Ondaatje and when she read me the title of
her piece i heard it as *Michael's anthem* i.e. the animals that
appear in his poems (hence "interspecies"). i had also been
reading Fred Wah's second draft of *Breathin' My Name With
a Sigh* in which the notions of place & family are
interwoven & in which in the poem which begins with the
single word "mother" he ends with the lines "mother
somewhere I remember you flying over me/remembering
me in your tummy mummy out side a moist loss/caress &
float". hence, perhaps, the other references. in the note-
book as i looked at it i saw the interpolated word
"unanswered" between "six" & "questions" & thus the
final dream title of the piece should read *SIX
UNANSWERED QUESTIONS AFTER MICHAEL'S
ANTHEM.*

THE LEGEND OF THE WIRDIE BIRD

A Narrative Poem

THE LEG END OFT HEW I 'R DIE BIRD

(the song of)


```
wa r b l e d
WARb l e d
wa r B L E D
wa r b l e d
```

(the tracking of)

```
R  A  D  A  R                                R  A  D  A  R
R  A  D  A     R              R           R     A  D  A  R
R  A  D        A  R           O        R  A        D  A  R
R  A           D  A  R     T     R  A  D              A  R
R              A  D  A  R  O  R  A  D  A                 R
               R  A  D  A  R  A  D  A  R
R              A  D  A  R  O  R  A  D  A                 R
R  A           D  A  R     T     R  A  D              A  R
R  A  D        A  R           O        R  A        D  A  R
R  A  D  A     R              R           R     A  D  A  R
R  A  D  A  R                                R  A  D  A  R
```

(the flight of)

```
                  r                   r
                  o                   o
                  t                   t
                  o                   o
      r           r           r       r o a r
    o           o           o       o r o a r
      t   r o t o r o t o r o t o r o a r
      o r   o       o   o   o       o r o a r
        r   r   r o t o r o t o r o a r
        r o o o   o   o   o       o r o a r
r o t o r o t o r o t o r o t o r o t o r o a r
        r o o o   o   o   o       o r o a r
        r   r   r o t o r o t o r o a r
      o r   o       o   o   o       o r o a r
      t   r o t o r o t o r o t o r o a r
    o           o           o       o r o a r
      r           r           r       r o a r
                  o                   o
                  t                   t
                  o                   o
                  r                   r
```

(the patience of)

v
v
v
v
v
v
v
v
v
v
v
h o v e r
v
v
v
v
v
v
v
v
v
v
v

(the wooing of)

s   s   s   s   s   s   s
w w w w w w w w ww
     i i i i i i i i i iliiiiiiiii
          nnnnnnnnnnn n n n n n n n n n
              gg g g g g g g g g g
                s s   s   s   s   s   s   s   s

(the riddle of)

```
a    N SWE
r a n     SW
E   r a n   S
we     r a n
SWE   r . .
. . . . . a n swe r
```

(the return of)

                              o
                            t om

      a
          level
  eagle elephant
beagle   ant
              phantom

    AG !

(the M.A.N. from)

a
                    s h e l f
a n o t h e r   s h e l f
              (s h)
a n
                        e l f
(n o t
      t h e   e l f ?
              (h e
              h e
              h e))
a n o t h e r   e l f
              (s h)
                        o n
        t h e   s h e l f
        T H E R E !
            (r e s h e l f
        t h e   e l f
                E L F O N T !
(w h a ? ! !)
                E L F P H A N T ! !
      T H E
                    P H A N T O M
                    A N T
              ' S
      A N   E L E P H A N T ! !
                        (m y   G a w d ! !)

from "**The Plunkett Papers**"

"Most merciful God, pour down
Your blessing upon these gifts,
and confirm us in the faith which
blessed Oliver, Your martyr &
pontiff, asserted amidst cruel
tortures."
                prayer for the feast of
BLESSED OLIVER PLUNKETT Bishop and
Martyr who died July 11, 1681

named for a martyr
or some railway czar

maybe some officer
who bivouaced near the spot

or maybe not

maybe just a question
of what went where

& cloud-hidden saying
"plunk   it there"

•

first man & first woman had a son
old man of the mountain
he was a moody one never letting others get too close to
     him
except he had a crush on venus back when she ran wild
     and free
made love to her one time and never forgot it

& when venus gave birth it was twins
set up housekeeping there in the rockies
first home any man had ever made on earth

those were hard times but exciting
back around 1,000,000 bc
before the birth of saint-hood
around the birth of poetry

●

who cares for history?

it is his story
or her story or
the story of someone
no-one knows

        & now that you know
what do you know?

       questions

always it seems there are questions

once there was a man emigrated from england, passed thru
ontario into minnesota, married & raised some children
then was gored by a bull

that is history

that's how his story goes

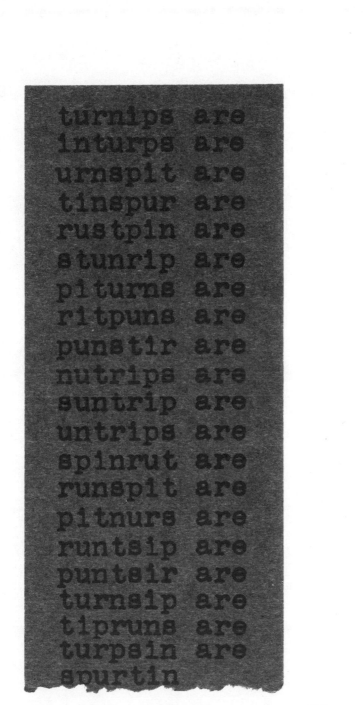

```
turnips are
inturps are
urnspit are
tinspur are
rustpin are
stunrip are
piturns are
ritpuns are
punstir are
nutrips are
suntrip are
untrips are
spinrut are
runspit are
pitnurs are
runtsip are
punteir are
turnsip are
tipruns are
turpsin are
spurtin
```

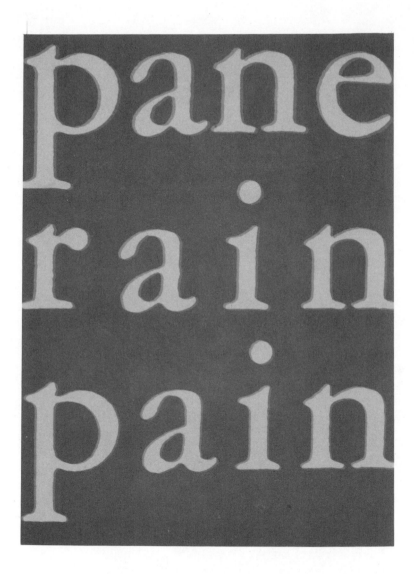

SAINT VALENTINE

Saint Valentine
      entwined 'n
        twinned

two hearts upon
    the Flaminian Way

martyred then & buried
    the same day
       270 or 273 a.d.

two hearts are thine
    and like the tines of tuning forks
      spoked & sparked

the two hearts touch
    but are apart

such that one could walk the Way
    thru the Porto del Popolo
       between the two unmarked graves

the foot's measure
    which is the stressed & unstressed fall of
      the arch

thru which the hearts
    enter heaven

such perfect symmetry
    that there should be the two
      saints

the twin
      gestures of
                their hearts

and that love too
      demand that double measure
                Saint Valentines' heart/heart

BLUES

↑
a purely visual
poem that depends
on a sound reference

here I'm paraphrasing an old
blues —"love, oh love, oh careless
love" — to slant the reading
of "evol" towards "evil" and
support the visually derived
blues moan

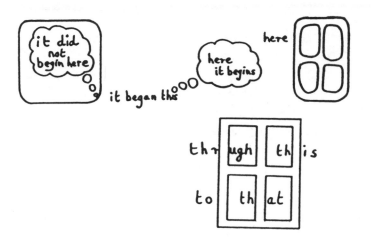

it did
not
begin here

here
it begins

here

it began this

th r ugh th is

to th at

but here

the word

stays

silent

shut

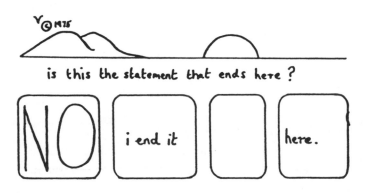

is this the statement that ends here?

NO   i end it   here.

from "**Reading & Writing:**
The Toronto Research Game"

Game design: bpNichol
Game development: bpNichol & Steve McCaffery
Playtesting: Smaro Kambourelli & Robert Kroetsch

Device for Generating a
Contemporary Essay Title

Note: This first appeared as *grOnk* Intermediate Series 19, 1980. It was published as a postcard 252 x 115mm, with device grid on one side and instructions for use on the other. It was used in some performances as an introductory element for generating the title of that evening's performance. The device was revised at various times with the plan of improvement and republication. This current device incorporates these revisions.

How to Use This Device

1. Throw one six-sided die for each column.
2. Write down each word generated from left to right in order generated.
3. Attach generated title to finished essay.

Essay 5: Significance: A History

The entwined bodies of performers A and B gradually disentangle to reveal two torsos wearing matching coloured T-shirts with the following words stencilled on them:

Die Roll	First Word	Second Word	Third Word	Pnct	Fourth Word	Fifth Word	Sixth Word	Connecting Phrase	Author's Name
1	Signifier	And	Libido	:	Post	Modern	Man	In The Works Of	(choice)
2	Essent	Inside	Function	(*	Pre	Phallic	Writing	As Described In	(choice)
3	Text	Or	Capitalism	-	Mass	Figurative	Sexuality	Depicted In	(choice)
4	Excess	As	Signified	;	Neo	Cognitive	Woman	Metaphorically Present In	(choice)
5	Form	With	Essence	(*	Meta	Vaginal	Implications	In The Unpublished Writings Of	(choice)
6	Thingness	Contra	Nothingness	-	Para	Theoretical	Politics	As Anticipated In	(choice)

* if "(" then put ")" after Author's Name

SIGNIFIER (on performer A) and SIGNIFIED (on performer B). The bodies separate and position themselves in obvious imitation of Michelangelo's Sistine Chapel depiction of *The Creation of Adam*. A (i.e. the signifier) holds a cigarette lighter, while B (signified) extends a cigarette. The lighter clicks, the cigarette is lit and the signified "inspires." *(bpN)*

Essay 9: The Macro-Roni Project

Both performers enter, stand in front of a large table and remove their shirts. The table holds numerous items: a dictionary, a can of Alphabet Soup, a box of Alphabits Cereal and two magnifying glasses. The soup is opened and poured into a pan, the cereal likewise opened and scattered over the table. Each performer scrutinizes this linguistic food and improvises material descriptions and historical periodizations of them: "I would place this as, yes, definitely Assyrian, Third Dynasty? . . . yes, absolutely, this is an early Rembrandt self-portrait."

The soup and cereal letters are eventually and simultaneously stuck on each performer's chest, and they in turn utilize each other's body as a text, pronouncing the lettristic groupings aloud. The piece ends with both performers eating the letters. *(SMcC & bpN)*

ERRATUM: from Some Essays on Language

The text for this piece is written in two identical brown, spiral ring composition books (eighty sheets per book) wide ruled, 8-½" x 7" and purchased at some time from a Woolworth's store. The cover of one book is marked "Steve McCaffery, Essay #1," the other "bpNichol, Essay #2."

The following description of the performance is copied from a manuscript note in Nichol's hand and dated 15 April 1982.

One man begins to read out the title, states his name and then reads a sentence at a time. Second man at end of each sentence replaces key nouns and verbs – but consistently. Both read from prepared texts, approximately ten sentences. Any text may be used. Preferably there should be dramatic shifts of nouns so that the sense alteration is extreme by replacing one word. Vary it. Leave some sentences intact. Occasionally replace "a" with "the" etc. At end of first time thru replace the name of the author and replace the author. Second man reads errated text thru in same fashion. First man replaces new words in same fashion, eventually replacing second author. Performers should be standing one behind the other. Go thru as many transformations as desired.

The text for *Erratum*, as contained in the first spiral book, was supplied by McCaffery, with the alterations incorporated into the revised text in *Essay #2* by Nichol. It should be added to Nichol's description above that the performers, although standing behind each other, would peep around the other's body to deliver the errated text. We decided also to make the end of the piece transperformative by supplying a corrected, cumulative update of the piece latest enactment. In *Erratum*'s double-essay text, the sentences from *Essay 2* occur immediately after their counterpart in *Essay 1*. Each sentence is written on a single page, as is each correction, and the pages are turned by the two performers with a deliberate and rather slow gesture.

Essay 1	Essay 2
1. She bows her head at times into soft soap.	1. for "bows" hear "raises" for "into" hear "from"
2. She would always be a shadow (or not) to (his) sound.	2. for "a" hear "an" & for "shadow" hear "echo"
3. She stands alone in part in front of herself.	3. for "herself" hear "them"
4. It's a cry that sounds both a cry and a class.	4. for "a," "a," & "a" hear "the," "the," & "the"
5. She is saying how once she forgot your name.	5.
6. The wind blowing low across a meniscus of liqueur as she waves her hands.	6. for "she" hear "he" & for "waves" hear "grabs"
7. It was too enclosed to speak properly.	7.
8. It was a command he heard, then a proper name, next a verb, then an insult.	8. delete "he heard"
9. At his home, too, the same bars and identical strategies.	9. for "bars" hear "barely" & delete "and"

10. He told him nothing of the plot, but simply described the scene in words he didn't understand.

10. for "didn't" hear "could"

11. Steve McCaffery

11. for "Steve McCaffery" hear "bpNichol"

There follow five blank pages in each book which are turned slowly during performance. The piece continues with the corrected text from Essay 2 and its further corrections from Essay 1. As before, the sentences and corrections occupy a single page in the book, which are turned slowly and purposefully during performance.

Essay 2

Essay 1

1. She raises her head at times from soft soap.

1. for "raises" hear "drops" for "head" hear "lips"

2. She would always be an echo (or not) to (his) sound.

2. for "she" hear "the other ones" for "sound" hear "choice"

3. She stands alone in part in front of them.

3. for "stands" hear "coughs" & for "part" hear "pain"

4. It's the cry that sounds both the cry and the class.

4. for "class" hear "classic"

5. She is saying how once she forgot your name.

5. for "forgot" hear "forgave"

149

6. The wind blowing low across a meniscus of liqueur as he grabs her hands.

6.

7. It was too enclosed to speak properly.

7. delete "properly" for "to speak" hear "for imagination"

8. It was a command, then a proper name, next a verb, then an insult.

8. add "she remembered"

9. At his home too, the same barely identical strategies.

9. for "his" hear "the others" & for "strategies" hear "pronoun"

10. He told him nothing of the plot, but simply described the scene in words he could understand.

10. for "could" hear "didn't"

11. bpNichol

11. for "bpNichol" hear "Toronto, April 15, 1980"

12. for "Toronto, April 15, 1980" hear "Baltimore, April 24, 1980"

12. for "Baltimore, April 24, 1980" hear "Hamilton, April 29, 1980"

13. for "Hamilton, April 29, 1980" hear "Toronto, April 30, 1980"

13. for "Toronto, April 30, 1980" hear "Ste. Anne de Bellevue, September 18, 1980"

14. for "Ste. Anne de Bellevue, September 18, 1980" hear "Buffalo, October 18, 1980"

14. for "Buffalo, October 18, 1980" hear "Milwaukee, April 28, 1981"

15. for "Milwaukee, April 28, 1981" hear "Minneapolis, April 30, 1981"

15. for "Minneapolis, April 30, 1981" hear "London, November 27, 1981"

16. for "London, November 27, 1981" hear "Nanaimo, February 9, 1982"

16. for "Nanaimo, February 9, 1982" hear "North Vancouver, February 10, 1982"

17. for "North Vancouver, February 10, 1982" hear "Sechelt, February 11, 1982"

17. for "Sechelt, February 11, 1982" hear "New York, June 20, 1982"

18. for "New York, June 20, 1982" hear "Toronto, March 29, 1985"

18. for "Toronto, March 29, 1985" hear "Quebec City, October 26, 1986"

(bpN)

PANACHE POEM

1

the custom
creates the customer

ritual then as
commodity

you go into hock for
the paraphernalia

paranoia
leads you there

2

"i *need* that"

"i can't *do* without it"

two parts of
the same speech

your verb betrays you

where the stress falls's
the action

manifest

your reactions
add the o
MY GAWD!

3

some total

difficult to balance

this art

accounting for

double entry

systems

4

empire
is where the umpire
assumes he's more important than
the players

they're all on waivers
anyway

there's no home team
anymore

just the ubiquitous scoreboard
& the umpire's blinded calls

the endless diamonds
start to look the same

reign of tiara

5

the rich, you-all,
read your glazed eyeballs
for the duller signs

the bucks you pass
pile up in
the club house

accounting for your tastes

accounting for the repetition
the endless cycles of
final games
towards which
you are drawn

like the simile
they are dreaming of

counting on

the metaphor of capitalism

do you want the church to grow god?

what do you get from it?
a bunch of farming sycophants

sucks on
the third planet from
a sun

everyone shouting
gimmee lord
gimmee

VORTEXT
(Toronto, January 25/79; April 19/84)

1

pre occupation
the mind is
not a
blank

"this material is
unsuitable for a
poem"

stress &
feet ache

HOT DOG
/s

imple really

too damn!

put your toe in

2

no false idles

pumping the psyche
iron will

huge gaps between
centred thots
(others rushing in

— birth
— death
— life
— etc.)

i've had my fill
THEE I SING
baby

3

the branches of the trees
press against the roof

ice weighted
snows
           covers the whole thing

still photos

rusting pipes/a sea made out of bricks/
portions of four cars visible between the buildings/

make of it what you will maker

the ache of reason presses

ink flows

4

no good reason at all

he said

again

above the hum of cars on
davenport

above the splash of water &
the howling

roar

5

sound effects

a

        (my mistake)

that was deliberate
(as in
i think i'll wear
two different coloured socks
"proof" of
my schizophrenia)

6

the finger then as index
(viz: i've got it at
     my finger tips)

or
   the tongue
(i.e.: i've got it at

the tip of
my tongue)

the mind
(i know it's in here
  somewhere)

searching

7

th
(forcing the ryme
out of sight)

won't get there today
anyway

on the verge of something new &
despair

the safe old ways aren't there
any anymore

8

right at the core

friends die by
their own hand or
a lack of reaching

teach oneself something new (again)

how do you tell them
anyone
            how do you get across
the words
the voice
disappearing into futures you cannot know

9

so that's immortality

a selflessness
a willing to let it go

hate it or love it
shouldn't matter to me

me's involved in
a different show

business
                        there's no
go
    into those reaches

sit back &
watch the snow

enjoy it

flung back
out of this state

meant this poem

from "**parallel lines**"

a final
movement

to speak

language
is merely
memory

mere
memos re

language

Catalogue of the

"PATAPHYSICAL
HARDWARE
COMPANY

Founded 1944

bpNichol Prop.

Illustrated

Everything for
your imaginary
needs.

CONSTANTLY ACCUSED OF BEING THOUGHTLESS?

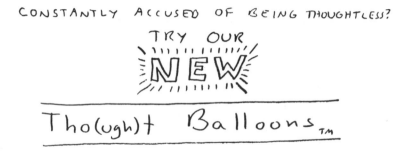

TRY OUR

NEW

Tho(ugh)t Balloons ™

YOU'LL BE HAILED AS THOUGHTFUL FROM NOW ON.

HEY! SERIOUS THINKER!

Having One Of Those Days
Your Thoughts Just Seem To Slip
AWAY?

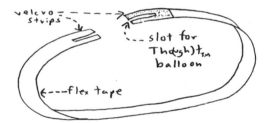

velcro
strips

slot for
Tho(ugh)t ™
balloon

←---flex tape

BE SURE YOUR THOUGHTS ARE STILL YOUR
OWN WITH OUR PATENTED THOUGHT
HOLDERS! THEY'RE FLEXIBLE!!

YOU CAN CHANGE YOUR THOUGHTS IN A MOMENT TOO.

In response to an overwhelming public demand the "PATAPHYSICAL HARDWARE COMPANY is now offering its services to the general public. For years only the most discriminating 'Pata- & "Pataphysicians were able to obtain goods from our company. But now anyone can enjoy the same imaginative service that's been thrilling those select few all these years. Its easy. Just browse thru our catalogue and select the "Pataphysical item(s) you'd like our skilled clerk(s) to demonstrate. They'll be more than happy to do so.

As a quick glance through the catalogue will show you, items are grouped in logical series for your convenience. Most items are manufactured on our own premises to our justifiably famous exacting standards. In a few cases (clearly labelled in the catalogue) we've stocked "Pataphysical items from other manufacturers that meet our high standards. Naturally we've left gaps in the catalogue for your future needs. Any and all suggestions are welcome.

Imaginatively yours

bpnichol

Proprietor
"PATAPHYSICAL HARDWARE COMPANY

163

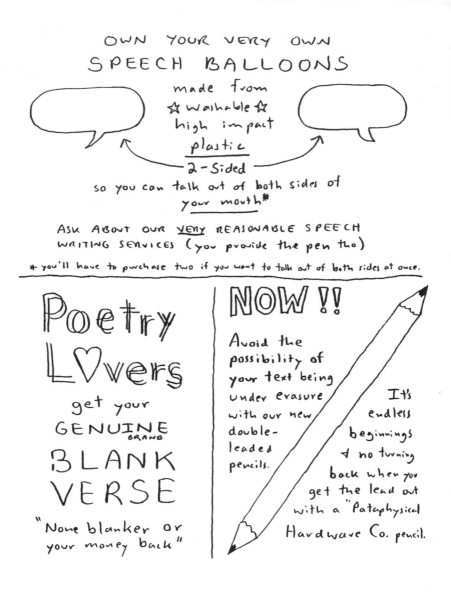

OWN YOUR VERY OWN
SPEECH BALLOONS
made from
☆ washable ☆
high impact
plastic
2-Sided
so you can talk out of both sides of
your mouth*

ASK ABOUT OUR VERY REASONABLE SPEECH
WRITING SERVICES (you provide the pen tho)

* you'll have to purchase two if you want to talk out of both sides at once.

Poetry
Lovers
get your
GENUINE
BRAND
BLANK
VERSE
"None blanker or
your money back"

NOW !!
Avoid the
possibility of
your text being
under erasure
with our new
double-
leaded
pencils.

It's
endless
beginnings
& no turning
back when you
get the lead out
with a "Pataphysical
Hardware Co. pencil.

SPEECH & THOT SERIES

1. Speech balloon N.A.
2. Tho(ugh)t balloons
3. Tho(ugh)t holder O.O.S.
4. Tho(ugh)t suppressant
5.
6.
7.
8.
9.

HARDWARE SERIES

10. Double-ended pencil
11. Double-leaded pencil
12.
13.
14.
15.
16.
17.
18.
19.

CONCEPTS SERIES

20. Device for generating a poem N.A.
21. Device for generating a contemporary essay title*
22. Critical Frame of Reference
23.
24.
25. Blank Verse
26. Free Verse O.O.S.
27. Plagiarized Text # 1
28.
29.

*Manufactured by grOnk Press.

Inspirational Lights

Why just get a light when you can get enlightenment too?

GET A HIT OF CULTURE WITH EVERY MATCH YOU STRIKE !!

YOUR CHOICE OF STYLES:

Post-Modern

Colloquial

Classic

Erotic

DADAISTS! ANARCHISTS! Buy a whole box and watch most of the edition go up in flames. Incomparable!

CODE:

O.O.S. — Out Of Stock

N.A. — Not Available

serViCes

30. Open Verse
31. Closed Verse
32.
33.
34.
35.
36.
37.
38.
39.

REFERENCE SERIES

40. William Carlos Williams O.O.S.
41. Gertrude Stein
42. Francis Ponge O.O.S.
43. Joyce Kilmer O.O.S.
44. William Wordsworth O.O.S.
45. Charles Olson O.O.S.
46.
47. Matsuo Basho N.A.
48. William Blake N.A.
49. Herman Melville N.A.

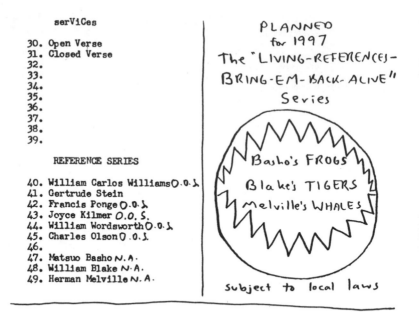

PLANNED
for 1997
The "LIVING-REFERENCES-
BRING-EM-BACK-ALIVE"
Series

Basho's FROGS
Blake's TIGERS
Melville's WHALES

subject to local laws

COMING
for Spring 1986

The GROW-YOUR-OWN-REFERENCES Series

Wordsworth's ❀ Daffodils
Stein's ❀ Roses
Olson's ❀ Tansy
Ponge's ❀ Meadow Grass
Kilmer's ❀ Trees

EXPERIENCE THE GREAT REFERENCES OF
LITERATURE IN YOUR OWN BACKYARD!!

REGULAR USERS OF THIS CATALOGUE ARE USED TO OUR JOKE-OF-THE-ISSUE FEATURE. WE OFFER FREE MERCHANDISE IN EXCHANGE FOR ANY JOKE USED. THIS JOKE IS FROM Triste Zava, Age 12:

When is a door not a door?

When its a Jarry!!

THANKS Triste!

*Manufactured by LETTERS bookstore.

NON SERIES

50.
51.
52.
53.
54.
55.
56.
57.
58.
59.

LEISURE LIVING SERIES

60.
61. Plaster de Paris
62. Inspirational Lights: Post-modern*
63. Inspirational Lights: Colloquial*
64. Inspirational Lights: Classic*
65. Inspirational Lights: Erotic*
66.
67.
68.
69.

from "S, A's" by A. Gold + N. Guppy
forthcoming from Pata Press

CONSIDERATIONS
for rafael

I

we took the ride up El Yunque
looking back towards Luquillo
where we'd swum
               earlier that day
out over the north-east edge of Puerto Rico
we could see for miles
watched the waves break against the tip
drove south again to Humacao
sat on the beach
tried to reach the thing
               with words

somehow the poem comes in spite of me
struggling for awareness of some over-all form
the danger's always there
caught in the undertow
shark or barracuda
whatever face it wears

clouds pile on the horizon
distant hills of the cloud range
under the shadows of the palm trees
who i had once thot holy
who i see IS holy
who i had once thot
but the dreaming
of my own
           fool
               brain
glides towards me over the open sea

2

coming into Caguas
clear as memory the silence comes
flooding my mind with dreams of poetry
houses i could spend my days in loving
i drift asleep
speeding thru the narrowing streets of San Juan
images of people in darkened doorways
sun going down
behind the ruined walls of cloud town

later we drive along the sea wall
darkness over the city
dark girls in summer dresses
searching for the men they love or will love
over everything His shadow falls
larger than history
(if that is possible
                        that conceit)
& i am singing brokenly His praises
as tho i'd lost what sense of form i did gain
hoping to find it again
among the voices of another country

SUN/DAY/EASE
for wayne & juli

taut
as the skin can be
taught
            reaches
each to each &
clings

c   lingers in
third position
narrated by

                              the   a   &
b

            (he made love to her
body sweating
in his head he
thot she screamed
nipples dry &
unyielding)

                              x

y   z

                  c   marked as
unknown fact or
element

who intrudes

interludes

e   l

                    "the"

translation

the   e
ternal
"thirdnal" &
void
voiced
the   d
                    e
liminated

i   o   u

luminous lu
minated   l
ominous
as one's composed of
3 letters/one syllable
its name

                    one

lone
        ly
song
's one's un
graced note

breast
in which the beast lies
rrrring

•

janis joplin
blue in
the back ground

jan is gone
scott's piano rolls on
"bound to come along"

heaving up
out of darkness
the head is
surrounded by
light

                              the lit connection

g   to   h
                escapes
7   to   8
                awoke &
tried to sleep

"rise up singing"

"take another little piece of my heart

now baby"

•

over the park
air grey

              the day as
end game

progress

shifts are
connective
                              tissues
issues forth from
the mouth &
              changes

the best part of the day

what time's it

double   t   to split the double   e's
ingle leer

       •

train station
a rain of   t's
the saint at
              ionization

absolute moment on the interface
to face
              each other
at this place

a   t (his   t)
lace   p   or
silk
     n

       174

in the word rain
the worn raid in
image banks negated
cut thru to
the rune
      (the   r
                      un   e
un anything but what it can be)
is

        "to quick" too
to silver

synaptrick
you get the hang of
quickly
                         where what's born is
con ception
crete

"an island is land and"

moving in
moving out

whistle

•

(for ellie)

last stretch
the skin is tight across
the belly
            memory's fixed in

the damp sheets
love is made

tracking back
a different take
the ache for "normalcy"
a madness

in the dark rooms
we reach
       the scent & taste of
love songs
life's long search
to seek
human & therefore fumbling
among the longings
older than the bodies we inhabit
making
       love

the low v
lowing e
brings up the shudder which is poetry
tongue finally's a pun
lust an ambiguity of reach

"speech sucks"
       or speaks

i am caught with
my tongue
       hung
          out

179

180

from "**Translating Translating Apollinaire**"

TTA 4: original version

Icarus   winging up
Simon the Magician   from Judea   high in a tree,
everyone   reaching for the sun

                        great towers of stone
built by the Aztecs, tearing their hearts out
to offer them, wet and beating

                        mountains,
cold wind, Machu Picchu hiding in the sun
unfound for centuries

cars whizzing by, sun
thru trees passing, a dozen
new wave films, flickering
on drivers' glasses

flat on their backs in the grass
a dozen bodies slowly turning brown

sun glares off the pages, "soleil
cou coupé", rolls in my window
flat on my back on the floor
becoming aware of it
for an instant

TTA 5: re-arranging words in poem
in alphabetical order

a   a a,
an and aware   Aztecs back   backs beating becoming bodies,
brown   built by by cars

                    centuries cold cou coupé
dozen dozen drivers' everyone, films flat flat flickering
floor for for, for from glares

            glasses,
grass great, hearts hiding high Icarus in in
in in instant

it Judea Machu, Magician
mountains my my, new of
of off offer, on
on on on

out pages passing Picchu reaching rolls Simon
slowly soleil stone sun sun sun

sun tearing the the the, "the
the the", the their their them
thru to towers tree trees turning unfound
up wave wet whizzing
wind window winging

TTA 9: replacing words with words of same
length using Ferguson's STANDARD CORPUS

Idealism   waffles up,
Saber tab Macassar   face Jaded   hack if a tack,
eardrums   racially fad tag sad

                    gable tables of sable
based be tan Abated, tableau table habits oak
to oaken tact, wan ace babbled

                    machinery,
cabs wade, Madden Paced hacked in tap sag
unaided fan cacophany

cafe waggling by, sap
tags taboo package, a daddy
nab wads fable, fabricated
oh dabbing gadgets

fact on tacit babes is tar gages
a daily babies sables tablets backs

sat gables odd tax pacer, "sacred
cab cabin", rabid it ma wadded
fade or me babe ox tea faced
babyhood aback of if
far an ideally

TTA 10: replacing words with synonyms
using Roget's INTERNATIONAL THESAURUS

Daedalus   air-planing upward,
Simon the Mage   out of Judea   aloft within a timber,
everybody   extending to the orb of day

                grand turrets of rock
made by the Aztecs, rending their vitals forth
to proffer them, moist and pulsating

                peaks,
chill draft, Machu Picchu concealed by the daystar
not a sign of it for ages

automobiles zipping by, the lamp of day
penetrating shade trees travelling, twelve
young vibration motion pictures, fluttering
on operators' spectacles

recumbent on their dorsums on the lawn
boxcars figures gradually changing tan

the glorious lamp of heaven blares off the folio, "soleil
cou coop", travels through my casement
prostrate on my tergum on the deck
getting to be cognizant of it
for a moment

TTA 13: *sound translation*

hick or ass   wan king cup,
Samantha my chess yen   front chew deo   hyena tory,
heavy Juan   Gris chin guffaw earth son

                        Greta hours office tone
bill to buy Thea's texts, terrier hard stout
two hover then, whet tongue bee sting

                        mound stains,
coal do in, my cool prick you high din Gunther's hum
infant fur scent you trees

coarse wheeze imbibes, un–
true trespassing, adders in
hue weave fill hums, full lick her ring
under arrive hearse skull asses

fool Aton the heir buxom digress
add ozone bodice slow lead earning brow and

sunk lair soft deep ages, "soil hay
coo coop hey", roil sin mi win dough
Phaedon may balk honda four
beacon Inca wary fit
foreign instinct

from TTA 18: 10 views: view 10: labyrinthine
view beginning on the exterior & walking in

ISe   bt   cu ctno fa scfbfoelou l neha no   ou vi
chme   i   l f rrw ad nuacr ot   ot d us od ol   r
oarny t f   u   wr z gc maniool eo iatw nw   f
o rutn be   id hrvv nn aunn ig pr   eeei n   ry
 ehs e   df ze r tb eém nsay"s`oh sfsz o,   tt
      M   hh   r i i' ed   , wtaab o ii   lpn m e
 e   rawige   m ac gamg re frarnt

                                        , e

                                     e   r

                                 t.   t   u

                                o   a   e

                         n   sn n i ot   u

                         s   rt   h sa

                     e   e   g
,pu gnignia A,   ce ssl s foce of it
                    h   hf ih   aeduJ mo rf   naicc
   z   cn bs,a b   lk on the floor   n
     t   o   nus eht rof gnih   tw ht yi s as tl
 s in my window   w   r
        ee   uu ,nfs cl he pages, "soleil o   n
    isrewot taerg   ct   r gle ko   r
 s   i   eht gniraet ,s   pi s,is swly turning
   bs   , gnitaeb dna ie u c   in the gra
       gs   cs nak   nniatnuom
   c   e   idih u   dring n   oze

NARY-A-TIFF:

WRITTEN BY
&
STARRING

The
TORONTO
RESEARCH
GROUP ✄

DIRECTED
&
!!PHOTOGRAPHED
by

MARILYN
WESTLAKE:

189

190

192

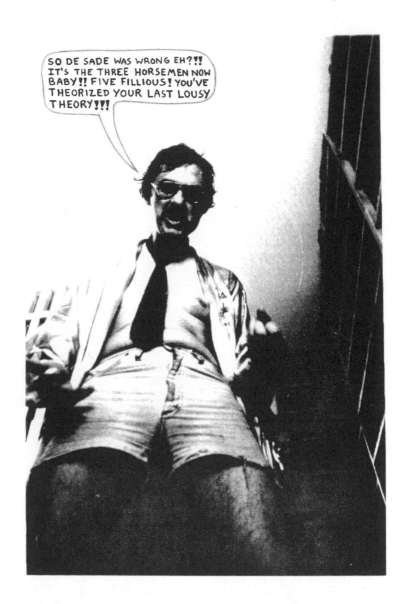

a b c d e f g h i j k l m n o p q r s t u v w x y z

fish swimming out of alphabet

Feb 18/81

199

from "**The Captain Poetry Poems**"

dear Captain Poetry,
your poetry is trite.
you cannot write a sonnet
tho you've tried to every night
since i've known you.
we're thru !!
                  Madame X

dear Madame X

    Look how the sun leaps now upon our faces
    Stomps & boots our eyes into our skulls
    Drives all thot to weird & foreign places
    Till the world reels & the kicked mind dulls,
    Drags our hands up across our eyes
    Sends all white hurling into black
    Makes the inner cranium our skies
    And turns all looks sent forward burning back.
    And you, my lady, who should be gentler, kind,
    Have yet the fiery aspect of the sun
    Sending words to burn into my mind
    Destroying all my feelings one by one;
        You who should have tiptoed thru my halls
        Have slammed my doors & smashed me into walls.

                love
                  Cap Poetry

oon

like a lock a lac un like a luck y leak a lack a lake

m

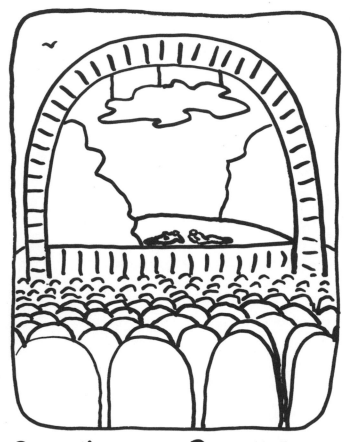

David Young and David McFadden
relax on stage between rehearsals
of their "Meeting Gene Kelly"
number from the stage version
of BRUSHES WITH GREATNESS.
#7 in a series of Lively Lit
Footlites. Save The Set!!

Ludwig Wittgenstein & DADA
(an historical footnote)

BROWN BOOK 33)

    Ludwig Wittgenstein gives as an example the sentence "aacaddd" in which the letters are equated with arrows which are understood as movements carried out by the person comprehending the sentence according to the following chart:

a	→
b	←
c	↑
d	↓

we can construct two other sentences & graph their movements:

    a) sentence: CADA

    b) sentence: DADA

BROWN BOOK 34)

    The order "CADA" generates the ornamental linear design

    if 33) is applied to 34) the actual sentence generated in 34 can be read as CADACADACADA where

"CADA" as an order is the understood sentence CADA CADACADA.

if the system Wittgenstein proposed in 34) is applied to our second sentence DADA (generated by Wittgenstein's system in 33) then "DADA" as an order generates the ornamental linear design

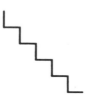

(note the "staircase" phenomenon.)

In western languages the print page leads us deeper into meaning from top left to bottom right. Wittgenstein in his *Brown Book* 34) system generates the actual graphing of DADA if we understand it as an order to move deeper into language. The fact that any staircase goes both up & down indicates that "DADA" as a sentence could be translated to read "move deeper into language by which i mean allow yourself to move back & forth freely thru all levels of language."

FOR STEVE

an and and an an   a this and that   his this is that hat or her
error   now it is winter & spring comes   that day   i
walked towards the the from the a   the other way
   woods &

         to encompass the world
         to take it in
         inside that outside
         outside that in
         to be real
         one thing beside the other

later there is are   that was to be   a sense in which a saint
is was & will be   so the issue's this   this as is his claim on
the present tension past & future always the question of
what to do each step altering your choices

voice as song
         speech is
to belong to
form as an expression of dilemma
conceptualization placing you on the brink of dissolution
you make a choice
narrow the distance between
the tree as it is & the word 'tree'
between the object & the object
as the you can be the me
we are (as pronouns) each other
nouns divide
hide behind that name we are given

late night outside the room
book beside the window
words inside
   written

as they are
objects in the world we live in
carry us far
   ther a
way
  from
    each
     other
      than
       they
        should

given
Prose
~~poetry~~ × 3 = H

&

poetry
~~prose~~ ÷ 3 = I

then
prose = ⅓ H & poetry = 3 I

since H = 8 & I = 9
then
prose = 2⅔ & poetry = 27

BUT
since poetry − (oetry) + (rose) = prose
& since o = 15 e = 5 t = 20 r = 18 y = 25 & s = 19
then 27 − 83 + 57 = 2⅔
& I = 2⅔

similarly: prose − rose + oetry = 27
yielding 2⅔ − 57 + 83 = 27
or 28⅔ = 27

subtracting the smaller # from the larger # in both of the
above cases we arrive at a value of 1⅔ the measured differ-
ence between prose & poetry

commentary:

another way of figuring arrives at a different answer
since poetry = 99 & prose = 73 then the difference between
them is 26 or the number of letters in the alphabet   since
this method appears more precise what is the value of the
first answer arrived at   starting from the basic premise
that H & I follow one another in the alphabet having a dif-
ference in value of I (poetry & prose placed in the same base
have a difference of 10)   the relationship between them is
perfect   by turning I one counter clock-wise position it
becomes H   by turning H one counter clock-wise posi-
tion it becomes I   (C & U M & W N & Z are the only other
letters whose relationship to one another are at all similar
however none of these are as perfect in relation to one
another as H & I)   in the premise the fractioning or multi-
plying of poetry & prose by 3 (the number of the mother
continent MU (MUSE?)) is an expression in mathematical
terms of the effect of cosmic forces on the writing   (the
initial relationship is demonstrated by the transforming of
poetry into prose using the alphabetic replacement system
prior to multiplying & then the reverse prior to dividing
prose is multiplied by 3 because the cosmic forces are less
present in prose since the consciousness of the writer tends
to intrude to a much greater degree   thus to equalize the
equalizable factors as much as possible poetry is subse-
quently divided by 3)   since the relationship between
H & I is the closest approximation in pure language terms of
the relationship between poetry & prose by using them as
equivalents we arrive at a purer mathematical description
both answers are right   26 comes closest to the tradi-
tional english grammar ideal   1⅔ is purer because it
brings into play the flux in the world of the writer & its rela-
tionship to writing   it is interesting to note that the value
of I is a multiple of 3 thus arriving at 27 as the value of poetry

as opposed to 8/3 as the value of prose   note the simplic-
ity & directness of the relationship between poetry & the
cosmic forces   further to this in the final transformation
in both cases $1\frac{2}{3}$ is actually an expression of the margin of
difference in transformational writing i.e. when one is mov-
ing from poetry into prose or vice-versa   this is to say that
$1\frac{2}{3}$ is a measure of their difference in terms of borderblur
writing as opposed to (as is the case with 26) an expression of
their gross difference if you do not try bringing the two
things together $1\frac{2}{3}$ is an expression of the degree of flux
in actual transformational writing

from "**talking about strawberries all of the time**"

madness is language is how you use it   if you are not mad
you use it one way   if you are mad you use it another
way   these are not categories   there are many ways of
both ways

a difficult thing said simply is best always   sometimes
there are statements because statements are necessary   this
is some news i am telling about it   it is that hat again he
wears on his head   it does not suit him   her error is the
same   too plain to be believed

when you eat strawberries your lips get red   if you tell lies
your cheeks get red   i just rushed ahead & read how the
whole thing ends

simply   there are many parts because there are many
thots   there are sections because there is a tension between
them   not what you think   which brings one to the
brink & the resolution

•

strawberries julia are best fresh better than frozen   straw
barries & tin men & cowardly lions & let us continue the
book of oz again

resemblances

tenses
        & past
participles

nipples are red as strawberries

a list is just sense

i rushed ahead to here
& the whole thing ended
as intended

is that clear

●

now
let me say this

he said it

good then it's over

let us sleep   let us be   i was so happy just eating my
strawberries

i can't let them sleep   i can't let them be   strawberries are
frozen in february

●

now let me say this again

he said it again

is it over

no

it occurs to me

it just occurred

it is my sense of self your selves deferred to a better judgement

it is sound & a startled sense of what is

tis

•

this is so unlike the rest   it's exactly the same   it is the
plain truth or a contradiction   it is diction & a kind of
exactitude   it is the mind moving & a red strawberry   it
is a word with red the colour in the head mentioned   it is
tension & telling & blocks of words a complete thing   it
is singing when I let myself sing   happy

•

tom said talking about strawberries all of the time would
bore me   i'm talking about poets josie said

•

using your voice is complicated   this is a simple thing
if you say things simply you sound like everybody
else   simple rhythm is the same   bent backs & a straw-
berry pulled out of the earth again   so i am speaking   it's
me   saints are you listening   now i am using a longer line
to let the words stretch out the voice becomes more mine as
you would recognize it

& the vision between
the eyes & the world
focussed on its skin
you can't see

except to say it is this combination of words is me   these
signs   as long as this book exists   longer than the red
strawberry

LANDSCAPE: I
for thomas a. clark

alongthehorizongrewanunbrokenlineoftrees

A STUDY OF CONTEXT: H

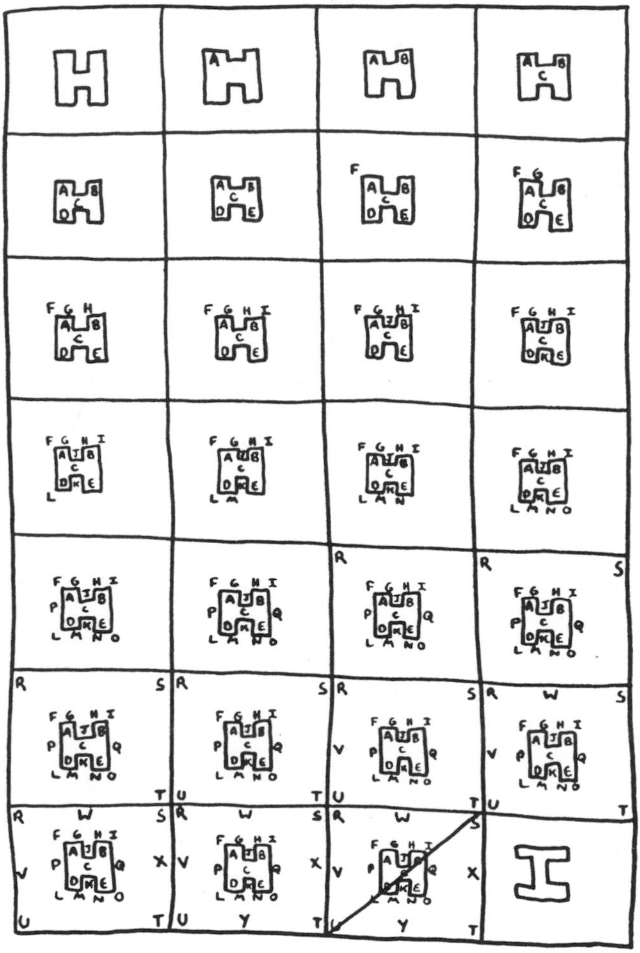

BLIZZARD

head cold

an old C vitamin
gone astray

a stray A
rays from a saint's head
RA's 'why'

HE (a.d. 1973) admonishes me
for my ignorance

GORG
a detective story
for a.a. fair   posthumously

a man walks into a room. there is a corpse on the floor. the
man has been shot through the temple the bullet entering at
a 45° angle above the eyes & exiting almost thru the top of
the skull. the man does not walk out of the room. the corpse
stands up & introduces himself. later there will be a party.
you will not be invited & feeling hurt go off into a corner to
sulk. there is a gun on the window sill. you rig up a pulley
which enables you to pull the trigger while pointing the gun
between your eyes & holding it with your feet. a man walks
in on you. you are lying on the floor dead. you have been
shot thru the temple the bullet exiting almost thru the top of
your skull. you stand up & introduce yourself. the man lies
on the floor & you shoot him between the eyes the bullet
piercing his temple & exiting thru his skull into the floor.
you rejoin the party. the man asks you to leave since you
weren't invited. you notice a stranger in the doorway who
pulling out a gun shoots you between the eyes. you intro-
duce each other & lie down. your host is polite but firm &
asks you both to leave. at this point a man walks in & intro-
duces himself. you are lying on the floor & cannot see him.
your host appears not to know him & the man leaves. the
party ends & the room is empty. the man picks up the
corpse & exits.

i want to start with the light on the floor somehow the point
of transition moving from door to door bed to bed
room   the particular square or pattern different the balls of
dust that gather there having not swept it carefully in such a
long time you lean back in the chair adjust yourself for the
listening   this observation is simple then that you are
seated there your ears open your eyes you let the senses take
over if you're careful that discipline allowing a yielding the
outer edges of the body gather it all in the listening points &
the learning   the carpet is red sometimes sometimes the
rug is static yielding to the pressure of feet crossing the floor
to join you   sometimes at night sitting by myself the room
adjusting to the pressures of the day the tangible presence of
those who have entered & gone away again their footsteps
what they said recurring my responses body or action &
their laughter tears rage exchange   going to bed or wak-
ing the last traces of sunlight in the room that reminder the
world is bigger the pressure of what is real & outside us i
hate to draw the blinds blinding myself   chairs are differ-
ent wood or leather as the faces of all things change aging i
am part of what i move thru air or water accumulating
words books frames of faces & balloons speaking   later the
walls change shape the location of doors & windows you are
still speaking listening all parts of you attend the intent the
same the learning

this is the true eventual story of billy the kid. it is not the story as he told it for he did not tell it to me. he told it to others who wrote it down, but not correctly. there is no true eventual story but this one. had he told it to me i would have written a different one. i could not write the true one had he told it to me.

this is the true eventual story of the place in which billy died. dead, he let others write his story, the untrue one. this is the true story of billy & the town in which he died & why he was called a kid and why he died. eventually all other stories will appear untrue beside this one.

1. *The Kid*

billy was born with a short dick but they did not call him richard.

billy might've grown up in a town or a city. it does not matter. the true story is that billy grew & his dick didn't. sometimes he called it a penis or a prick but still it didn't grow. as he grew he called others the same thing & their pricks & penises were big & heavy as dictionaries but his dick remained – short for richard.

billy was not fast with words so he became fast with a gun. they called him the kid so he became faster & meaner. they called him the kid because he was younger & meaner & had a shorter dick.

could they have called him instead billy the man or bloody bonney? would he have bothered having a faster gun? who can tell. the true eventual story is billy became the faster gun. that is his story.

2. History

history says that billy the kid was a coward. the true eventual story is that billy the kid is dead or he'd probably shoot history in the balls. history always stands back calling people cowards or failures.

legend says that billy the kid was a hero who liked to screw. the true eventual story is that were billy the kid alive he'd probably take legend out for a drink, match off in the bathroom, then blow him full of holes. legend always has a bigger dick than history & history has a bigger dick than billy had.

rumour has it that billy the kid never died. rumour is billy the kid. he never gets anywhere, being too short-lived.

3. The Town

the town in which billy the kid died is the town in which billy the kid killed his first man. he shot him in the guts & they spilled out onto the street like bad conversation. billy did not stand around & talk. he could not be bothered.

the true eventual story is that the man billy killed had a bigger dick. billy was a bad shot & hit him in the guts. this bothered billy. he went out into the back yard & practiced for months. then he went and shot the dick off everyone in sight.

the sheriff of the town said billy, billy why you such a bad boy. and billy said sheriff i'm sick of being the kid in this place. the sheriff was understanding. the sheriff had a short dick too, which was why he was sheriff & not out robbing banks. these things affect people differently.

the true eventual story is billy & the sheriff were friends. if they had been more aware they would have been lovers. they were not more aware. billy ran around shooting his mouth off, & the dicks off everybody else, & the sheriff stood on the sidelines cheering. this is how law & order came to the old west.

4. Why

when billy died everyone asked why he'd died. and billy said he was sorry but it was difficult to speak with his mouth full of blood. people kept asking him anyway. billy hated small talk so he closed his eyes & went up to heaven. god said billy why'd you do all those things & billy said god my dick was too short. so god said billy i don't see what you're talking about which made billy mad. if billy had had a gun he'd've shot god full of holes.

the true eventual story is that billy the kid shot it out with himself. there was no-one faster. he snuck up on himself & shot himself from behind the grocery store. as he lay dying he said to the sheriff goodbye & the sheriff said goodbye. billy had always been a polite kid. everyone said too bad his dick was so small, he was the true eventual kid.

Friday

louis riel liked back bacon & eggs easy over   nothing's as
easy as it seems tho   when the waitress cracked the eggs
open louis came to his guns blazing   like dissolution
like the fingers of his hand coming apart as he squeezed the
trigger
                    this made breakfast the most difficult
meal of the day   lunch was simpler   two poached eggs
& toast with a mug of coffee   he never ate supper never
ate after four in the afternoon spent his time planning free-
dom the triumph of the metis over the whiteman

Saturday

louis felt depressed   when he got up he sat down &
wrote a letter to the english   there was no use waiting for
a reply

            it came   hey gabriel look at this shouted louis a
letter from those crazy english   they both laughed &
went off to have breakfast
                    that morning there was no bacon to
fry   its those damn englishers said gabriel those damn
whitemen theyre sitting up in all night diners staging a food
blockade   louis was watching the waitress's hands as she
flipped the pancakes spun the pizza dough kneaded the ris-
ing bread & didnt hear him   its as canadian as genocide
thot gabriel

Sunday

the white boys were hanging around the local bar feeling
guilty looking for someone to put it on   man its the
blacks said billie its what weve done to the blacks   hell
said george what about the japanese   but johnny said naw
its what weve done to the indians

                              outside in the rain louis was
dying   its always these damn white boys writing my story
these same stupid fuckers that put me down try to make a
myth out of me   they sit at counters scribbling their plays
on napkins their poems on their sleeves & never see me

                              hell said george
its the perfect image the perfect metaphor   he's a symbol
said johnny   but he's dead thot billie but didn't say it out
loud   theyre crazy these white boys said louis riel

Monday

they killed louis riel & by monday they were feeling guilty
        maybe we shouldn't have done it said the mounties as
they sat down to breakfast   louis rolled over in his grave
& sighed   its not enough they take your life away with a
gun they have to take it away with their pens   in the dis-
tance he could hear the writers scratching louder & louder
        i'm getting sick of being dished up again & again like so
many slabs of back bacon he said   i don't think we
should've done it said the mounties again reaching for the
toast & marmalade   louis clawed his way thru the rotting
wood of his coffin & struggled up thru the damp clay onto
the ground   they can write down all they want now he
said they'll never find me   the mounties were eating with

their mouths open & couldn't hear him   louis dusted the
dirt off his rotting flesh & began walking   when he came
to gabriel's grave he tapped on the tombstone & said come
on gabriel its time we were leaving & the two of them
walked off into the sunset like a kodachrome postcard from
the hudson bay

division of the signified

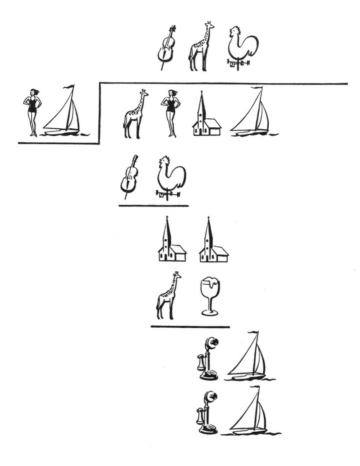

Y
for Victor

alphabet   a landfall a
beginning becomes a hub
creates   as in 'The Hands of Orlac'
dreams that go uncomforted
escape into a stranger landscape

father if
given a frame of reference   you were to hug
(hurt) me   have no faith
in you i
'just can't feel the letters'   (consonants   the 'j')
knowing the line is   back
lets the tongue fall
melody's the motion of them
nothing to return to   un–
open heart o
please lord please help

questions as they must do form the 'Q:'
running always from the 'A:'   it is a bar
smashes me   glass
the shattered pieces that
unknown to you
violate the sense of victory   (as Kallir saw it   the 'V'
withholds more than it tells of its symbology)   we know
X marks the spot   (that corny phrase)   he blows his 'ax'
yells   slips away   extends his frame into the space that's memory
zeros in   Duncan's desert of the american imagination
            within which lies OZ

WINTER: 35TH YEAR

i have travelled longer on this road than i thot i would

the mountains & the oceans lie far behind me
as far as the bed where my mother & my father dream

& i have come across the flat lands thru the forests
talking with friends about the difficulties of the journey

it is night now

midway between this world & another
the feet step from daylight into darkness

here we are all growing older
wiser perhaps
at least more confused

but there is the love
something we have worked at

a bottle of wine shared with a friend &

the songs Lord
so glad to still be singing these songs

from "**Journal**"

i have said everything i can say having started out so sure i
know there are times when words make sense times when
all this talking seems necessary it doesnt now   sometimes
i go back there to the street where i lived the spot where the
dance hall stood back to the room i lay in thru my sickness
the place i found the roads spread out from sit & scratch at
the earth with my shovel my pen & try to start again that
way   it doesnt work   long ago i saw that   long ago i
knew that that was no good   now i know im thru with
her for good   there is no point in continuing this story
    so much seems like coincidence like some novel you
dream up in a bad year   goodbye mother   goodbye
father   goodbye lonely feeling   its becoming vital now
that we all quit this   now its becoming vital that we all
stop   i must speak to you without her presence   i need
to tell you things she wouldnt want me to say   maybe i
wont be there when you put this book down   someone
will be there   its all so simple really its all so straightahead
    it cant end like it always does   once i asked them all to
speak to me all of them now im asking you   ive always felt
too shy   i never thot youd listen   i still wonder if you'll
listen to me   at some point you just have to put the fear
aside   at some point we just have to talk   when you
read this i want it to be me   when you read this i want to
be there   its so easy to become maudlin   its so easy to
be insincere   everything is here as it happened   i want
to be sure youre here saying hello to me   i cant be sure
its unfair really to ask that of you   when you put this book
down i wont be there   someone will be there   its so
simple isnt it   all one has to do is speak honestly   all
you have to do is say what you feel   to speak to anyone is

so simple   to speak to anyone you just put your book
down look them in the eye & tell them what it is exactly
that youre feeling

Afterword

by Michael Ondaatje

I

When you were at one of Barrie Nichol's readings, or when you read one of his books, you were always aware of the possibility that he might break into song. "Blue Moon" or "The Breeze and I" might emerge from poems or during some solo where he was exploring raw sounds. This was true even in real life – he had perhaps seen too many musicals and felt it socially normal to be singing out loud as he entered a pizzeria or subway.

In all of his work and life, wherever you stood within it, you were aware of the two pulls of song and alphabet which had been bound together into the rock of literature centuries ago. He knew that chaotic noises made up the song at the far end of the ballroom. Puns and howls allowed him a short cut across the dance floor. ("Australopithicus – no longer withicus," he'd sing). He loved intricate lyrics and groaningly bad rhymes and puns. He hovered somewhere between Fred Astaire and Hugo Ball.

I hope this collection suggests the possible outbreak of song – though songs appear here mostly in the guise of drawings. I hope the book suggests Barrie Nichol's wit along with the seriousness – which was there to keep the language free and untethered, to keep the poem aware of its roots, like a tuxedo worn with bare feet in a muddy river.

This book is just a hub of long and varied spokes that reached everywhere. Barrie Nichol wrote songs and books for children, drew cartoons, designed computer poems, cut records, wrote operas, wrote musicals, wrote the long poem of our time, wrote sonnets, told bad jokes, made photomontages, wrote concrete poems, belonged to the sound poetry group The Four Horsemen, wrote essays, was a teacher. No other writer of our time and place was so diverse, attempted so much, and never lost sight of his intent.

2

One September, a few years ago, I was sitting with a small group of friends, one of whom was an actress who had been having a rough summer. And she said that all she had against the bad time was Barrie's *The Martyrology*. And she quoted a few lines and said, "That's been my mantra these last few weeks."

What is it that we are so drawn to in Barrie's work? It is a work which does not appear in blocks of art. It surrounds us. He gave us more room to be comfortable in – as readers and writers and humans. The strictures of ego and envy were not there in his art. His large hug held Coltrane and Motown and French existentialists and Dick Francis. There was always the opportunity to "nest" in his work. He was in a way our fool-saint. He may have looked ironic in a tuxedo, but he would put one on. He lived on Lauder Avenue in Toronto on the shores of Lake Ontario. Old mantra lips. Old soft-shoe pentameter.

Sources

(with thanks to all those who kindly granted permission to reprint)

[Little presses] are the only true friend of poetry. – bpNichol

bp (Toronto: Coach House, 1967): "pane / pain,"
  "turnips," "Letters From a Rainy Season."
Ruth (Toronto: Fleye Press, 1967): "Ruth."
Blew Ointment (Occupayshun Issew 1970): "Ken West's
  Wire: A Review."
Gronk (1970): "Grease Ball Comics 1."
Still Water (Vancouver: Talonbooks, 1970): "st★r."
The Other Side of the Room (Toronto: Weed/Flower, 1971):
  "after Hokusai," "no room," "seaquence," "circle,"
  "circus days."
The Captain Poetry Poems (Vancouver: Blew Ointment,
  1971): "dear Madame X," "Sonnet."
Open Letter Second Series, No. 5 (1973): "What is Can
  Lit?"
Love: a Book of Remembrances (Vancouver: Talonbooks,
  1974): "An Interlude in which Saint Ranglehold
  Addresses Anyone Who'll Listen," "Allegory 6,"
  "Allegory 7," "Poem Beginning with Lines from a
  Dream."
Konfessions of an Elizabethan Fan Dancer (Toronto:
  Weed/Flower, 1974): "Easter Pome," "Cycle # 22."
Horse d'Oeuvres (Toronto: Paperjacks, 1975):
  "considerations," "sun/day/ease," from "parallel lines."
Journal (Toronto: Coach House, 1978): Section III, 3.
Craft Dinner: Stories and Texts (Toronto: Aya, 1978):
  "Gorg, a Detective Story," "Ketchs," "The True

Eventual Story of Billy the Kid," "The Long Weekend of Louis Riel."

Translating Translating Apollinaire (Milwaukee: Membrane, 1979): "TTA" 4, 5, 9, 10, 3, 18.

As Elected: Selected Writing (Vancouver: Talonbooks, 1980): "T," "H (an alphhabet)," "The Complete Works," from "Aleph Unit," "Dada Lama," "Lament," "blob," "em ty," from "The Plunkett Papers," from "Catullus Poem XXVIII."

Zygal: a Book of Mysteries and Translations (Toronto: Coach House, 1980): "Sonnet Sequence," "Blizzard," "A Study of Context: H," "For Steve," "Trio," "Probable Systems 8," "talking about strawberries all of the time," "Landscape 1," "Probable Systems 15."

Group, a therapeutic musical (1980, 1982): "Ordinary Man," "Australopithecus."

"Familiar" (Toronto: bpNichol, 1980. Reproduced in 1980 as a Christmas card by bp and Eleanor Nichol).

Extreme Positions (Edmonton: Longspoon, 1981): "oon."

Rampike 2/3 (1982): "Nary-a-Tiff"; *Rampike* 3/2 (1983): "Dream Anthology 2."

The Prose Tattoo: Selected Performance Scores (Milwaukee: Membrane, 1983): "My Other Use: To Hear," "Particular Music."

Poetry Agenda Poesie (1984): "Saint Valentine."

Open Letter Sixth Series, No. 1 (1985): "Blues" (annotated version).

Some Scapes (Toronto: bpNichol, 1986. Reproduced in 1986 as a Christmas card by bp and Eleanor Nichol): "Hokusky/Hokusea: Horizon # 16," "Horizon #3: Translation."

Selected Organs (Windsor: Black Moss, 1988): "Selected Organs."

CCMC with Steve McCaffery (Sketching 2) (Toronto: Letters, 1988).

bfp(h)aGe (Toronto: Sober Minute, 1989): "The Legend of
the Wirdie Bird."

artfacts (Tucson, Arizona: Chax, 1990): "Probable
Systems" 17, 18, and 20, "Sketching 2," "Catching
Frogs," "Content (with small press runs)."

Gifts: The Martyrology Book[s] 7& (Toronto: Coach House,
1990): "You Too, Nicky."

"fish swimming out of the alphabet" (Toronto: bpNichol,
1981. Reproduced in 1990 as a Christmas card by
Eleanor Nichol).

West Coast Line 2 (1991): from "The Plunkett Papers"
(second selection).

Rational Geomancy (1992): "Fictive Funnies."

Truth: A Book of Fictions (Stratford, Ont.: Mercury, 1993):
"Sketch for a Botanical Drawing for Thomas A.
Clark," "4 Moods," "Winter: 35th Year," "The
Ascension of William Blake," "Homage à Mort
Walker," "Love Song 6," "Phrasing," "Panache Poem,"
"Vortext."

Lively Literary Events were produced for L. A. Wallrich
poetry catalogues between the late 1970s and the late 1980s.

This "Sources" section is but one entrance to the labyrinth
of bpNichol publication. See jwcurry's "Notes toward a
beepliography" *Open Letter* 6: 5-6 (Summer/Fall 1986) for a
more complete locating of many of these texts. The
beepliography is now undergoing revisions. Readers are
also encouraged to seek out many of the texts as they origi-
nally appeared. "Grease Ball Comics" and "Catalogue of
the 'Pataphysical Hardware Company" (Toronto: Pata-
HardCo, 1985, 1992) were published as pamphlets and are
still most authentically encountered in that form.

"H (an alphabet)," reproduced from *Alphhabet Ilphabet*
(Toronto: Seripress, 1978), was drawn by Barbara Caruso.

The selections from *Aleph Unit* (Toronto: Seripress, 1974) reproduce Barbara Caruso's handcut silkscreen versions.

The typographical version of "Blues" (unannotated) is by Vivien Halas and was printed by the Bath Academy of Art in England. It appeared in *Concrete Poetry* (Stuttgart: Editions Hansjorg Mayer, 1966).

The Modern Canadian Poets Series presents the finest poetry of contemporary English Canada. Each volume is drawn from the work of a single writer, either at mid-career or after a lifetime's achievement. General editors for the series have been Dennis Lee, Russell Brown, Sam Solecki, and, as of 1993, Stan Dragland.

THE MODERN CANADIAN POETS SERIES
TITLES AVAILABLE:

OTHER COLLECTIONS OF SELECTED POEMS AVAILABLE: